Feelings Women Rarely Share

Judy Reamer

Feelings Women Rarely Share

Judy Reamer

Copyright © 1987, 2003 by Judy Reamer
Printed in the United States of America
ISBN: 0-9744231-1-4
Editorial Assistance
by Donna Cornelius

Scripture quotations are from the *King James Version* of the Bible unless otherwise noted.

Bible quotations **taken from** the *New American Standard Bible,* © The Lockman Foundation, 1960, 1962, 1963, 1968, 1971, 1972, 1973, 1975, 1977, are used by permission.

Bible quotations taken from the *New International Version,* © International Bible Society 1973, 1978, are used by permission.

5th printing (Newly Revised Edition) 2003.

Contents

Dedication

To Bernie, a one-in-a-million husband, and to Mark, Johnny, Jeff, and Jill, our four-in-a-million children, you gave me abundant "space" to author this book. You allowed me to be "single" in purpose. You cheered me on to the finish line before the book could finish me! May you reap well, for you have sown with rich seed. I love you as always and forever.

Foreword

Judy Reamer is as Jewish as Saul of Tarsus and as evangelistic as the transformed apostle Paul. Years ago, in Las Vegas, Nevada, I had the privilege of baptizing Judy as a believer in the Lord Jesus Christ. She came up out of the water filled with the radiance of heaven.

Since then, she and her family have grown in the Lord, become seasoned and knowledgeable in His Word, and used by God in showing others the way to life, both here and in the hereafter.

Writing this book has cost Judy and her family both time and a journey into adventure and emotion. But it has been a worthwhile journey!

I shed tears when I first read it, realizing how women everywhere vitally need this information. I understand women's feelings in general more clearly and appreciate more deeply my own wife Shirley. Only a Spirit-filled woman such as Judy Reamer could be equipped to share a woman's temptations as candidly as she has and to outline the answers provided by God.

I am sure that many outwardly successful but inwardly troubled women will be greatly helped by reading this book.

—Pat Boone

Beverly Hills, CA

"God's forgiveness is unrestricted. But sexual sins are worse in that they are more damaging personally and socially than all other sins. . . . our sexuality is so significant a part of our human nature that the sense of guilt over sexual sin is not easily released. . . ."[1]

—Jack Hayford

"The finest, most Spirit-filled and devoted Christians struggle with misdirected desire."[2]

—Tim Stafford

Prologue

Everything I needed to know regarding what *I didn't know* about immorality, I am learning as a widow.

At a conference fifteen years ago I began with, "I'll be teaching about immorality. You 'elderlies' out there, please bear with me and rejoice for the 'youngies' who may benefit from this teaching."

I felt I needed to apologize to those over sixty years old for my choosing the subject of lust for the meeting.

After the teaching a stocky, white-haired, rosy-cheeked woman came to the podium as I was gathering my props. "Judy, please don't ever apologize for teaching that subject to us older gals. We may be old, but we're not dead!" I knew she was sincere, but it seemed strange to me that a woman in her sixties would have a reason to be helped by *The Parable of the Chocolate Chip Cookie* (my presentation about immorality).

Now I am older *and* . . . I am a widow. When the book first came out, I was securely, snugly, and smugly married. I had always had someone to hold me in his arms, to squeeze my hand, to wink at me. I had someone waiting for me, waiting on me, and waiting to hang on my every word when I'd arrive home. (Bernie may have been a great actor!) What I miss most is his companionship and his always-accessible comfort.

Since originally published, this tiny book has become a bestseller. A small percentage of the readers have been single. I had written it primarily for those who found themselves *attracted to someone they couldn't have because they belonged to someone else.* Now that I have no one, I have a newly birthed empathy for those who are single by choice or circumstance. While a married woman, I was unaware of this magnified vulnerability in single women. Until I was no longer attached, this awareness of a powerful vulnerability would have been unattainable.

As I reread my original edition (I needed to for my own use!), I decided to let it remain almost intact because the book still speaks *life.* However, I wanted to let you know that as a fairly young widow, yet no longer a "youngie," I now have faced massive new struggles in this area. I am the better for it. I can now speak with more understanding, clarity, and appreciation for those sorely tempted, as romantic emotions are the same at age 16 as they are at age 106! We may see how the Bible treats lust in the following:

> You have heard that it was said, 'Do not commit adultery.' But I tell you that anyone who looks at a woman lustfully has already committed adultery with her in his heart (Matthew 5:27, 28 *NIV*).

The Bible treats lust as deadly serious. Right on the heels of those words comes:

> If your right eye causes you to sin, gouge it out and throw it away. It is better for you to lose one part of your body than for your whole body to be thrown into hell. And if your right hand causes you to sin, cut it off and throw it away. It is better for

you to lose one part of your body than for your whole body to go into hell (Matthew 5:29, 30 *NIV*).

In order to personally do what that scripture implied, I had to experience a powerful grace given to me by the Lord. The battle was one of the fiercest I've ever had. He brought me to a place where I'd rather be maimed than hurt this empathetic yet transcendent God. Yes, as a single woman, I have now lived through (or *died* through) being consumed with romantic emotions resulting in weight loss and sleepless nights. The caveat was that I was being drawn to someone who was not God's choice for my future. I am a widow old enough to adroitly hide my hair roots, but I'm not clever enough to hide from my Creator. I knew that any disobedience to God's individual plan for my future would break the intimacy with Him. The developing relationship between the *significant other* who had invaded my life and myself was fodder for God's dealings. This relationship had to be put on the death altar. Yes, Isaac was restored to Abraham, but we have to trust God who determines if it is Isaac or if it is an Amalekite, who *reeeeally* (!) needs to be destroyed.

The *surgical* choice of cutting off a relationship, which was not God's best for me, felt like death. In reality it was *life* for every sinew of my being. Yet, I didn't experience this *life* in the midst of making the choice. First I chose God above "the handsome prince," and then I was thrilled and surprised to taste the benefit of His tremendous peace.

The Revelation of Infatuation

"Some enchanted evening . . . you may see a stranger across a crowded room and somehow you know, you know even then, that somehow you'll see

her again and again."—Rodgers and Hammerstein,
South Pacific

Often there's a table laden with sweets offered
between retreat sessions. I'll glance at it for one
reason. Is there anything chocolate calling out to me?
Chocolate is loaded with a substance called phenyl
ethylamine (PEA). That chemical causes laboratory
rats to continually bear down on switches until fatigue
forces them to drop dead. As I am in love with
chocolate, I now understand there is a certain
chemistry going on between me and that rich brown
delicacy.

The craving for a genuine Toll House chocolate
chip cookie (loaded with chocolate chunks!) is similar
to the craving for romantic euphoria. Scientific
research indicates that when we find ourselves drawn
to the opposite sex, the exact amphetamine-like
chemical in chocolate is quickly triggered in the brain.
(Like flash, bam, alakazam!) This teeny tiny molecule
initiates a swift move of gossip-like information among
nerve cells.

A whirl of exhilaration ensues in the brain,
which lifts a simple attraction onto another plane. It's
as if the mundane victim becomes a Superman. This
exhilarating chemical enables the restful soul to
experience the assertive get-up and go! There's a
newly named syndrome called The Relationship
Addiction. People love the high.

I can see why God had to call PEA into
existence. If it weren't for the stupor of romance, why
would any man or woman want to get "hitched"?!?
Marriage is surrender, commitment, compromise, and
work. Oh, my!

Researchers are certain that this infatuation
chemical, PEA, behaves similarly to the illegal
addictive drug "Speed."

The drug of romance/lust causes some to yearn for it. PEA is the booster shot, which perhaps may be blamed for the continuation of the species. Who needs Cupid when we have this powerful molecule?

After exposing this potent scientific truth, I say there's no reason to discard the potent infatuation. Infatuation has its very important role to play in courtship and contributes to building a reliable intimate partnership. It's the first step toward . . . bona fide attraction.

The Path of Infatuation
Or Being a Fool for Love

In view of the fact that infatuation has an intoxicating hold over imaginations and our choices, let's familiarize ourselves with the path. The theory starts with a person beginning to hold your interest either by his words, his body language, a surprising kindness, the set of his jaw, his status in life, or the like.

Then you, the PEA-attacked person, spend time waiting for a phone call, watching for the mailman, waiting for the next (face to face) encounter. Unstoppable thoughts are intruding with a power all their own. These thoughts are solidifying the picture of this new interest. You begin to see this person as absolutely marvelous. He becomes bigger than life in his attributes, but you are totally blind to his failings. All appears so good; the future looks great with this person.

Sadly, you're accosted with the perpetual fear you may not be able to have what you want . . . him! Emotional seasickness becomes your sport of non-choice. You are consciously driven by simple fear. If you were to write a book, it would be entitled, *The Nauseating Dread of Not Acquiring What I Passionately Am Starting to Desire.* A long title, yes? In like manner, the days seem, oh so long, as you wait and hope for all your dreams to be fulfilled. This dread is the unique torment reserved for the infatuated elite.

The Primary Dynamics of Infatuation

High Expectation and Nail-Biting Uncertainty!

It reminds me of a flower arrangement which arrived one day. It was a dozen red *bud* roses with much promise. They hadn't yet opened, yet every few hours I'd think, *"They're going to open. They should open. Why wouldn't they open? They'd better open!"* The buds of promise never delivered. Ultimately, the world at large was left with a sorely frustrated and disappointed Judy! The buds of high promise pooped out. Not a particularly infrequent happening with red roses . . . and infatuation.

Ah, sweet chemistry. The chemistry course in high school was never very popular. It had a sorry reputation. It birthed lots and lots of Ds. Likewise, this PEA chemistry has birthed many "sick puppies" in the realm of romance.

Family therapist Dana Peach commented:

> Infatuation begins as an important emotional signal to point you in the direction of desire to get you moving toward a mate. But it is not yet love and its impetus will never take the place of thinking about what you want and acting persistently on that intention.

How does one use the above reflection to build a "sure foundation" in a relationship, or even to beat the *folly* at its game before the PEA clicks in?

The book *How to Know if Someone is Worth Pursuing in Two Dates or Less* written by Neil Clark Warren is one I highly recommend. It is to be "rubbed" on the mind before the first outing with a male, "soaked" into the fiber of your being before you answer the doorbell, "swallowed" before the romantic emotions start. (Take what you want from the book. It's a worthwhile read, spiritually practical.)

Additionally, to give yourself the best chance for God to use the following pages to protect and deliver you—

READ THIS ENTIRE BOOK.

A survey showed most people read a third of a book and lay it aside. . . . forever. What's in the second half of this book is extremely interesting and practical. Why the emphasis on my request? Because the three ways most of us are going to handle temptation will depend on:

- Spiritual maturity
- Self understanding
- Good training

For good training and instruction, a large number of people have told me this entire book is a valuable tool. If the following is any indication that what people say is true, here's just one of many letters confirming why I am urging you to go through the whole book.

Dear Judy,

I feel that God is leading me to write you. Over two years ago I attended one of your seminars. I can't say your words of Christian wisdom were life changing then, but today they are. I have gone on a much-needed spiritual retreat. I brought your book with me. Your words have changed my, life. God was speaking directly to me through you.

I've never done anything like this before but I feel such a strong sense of urgency to tell you how much God loves you. I have prayed that He will guide my pen—I can't seem to write fast enough.

I have written down one of your departed husband's favorite scriptures to help me get through the problems I am presently facing. I am memorizing the verse and keeping it with me for continual inspiration. I, too, want to apply Phil 4:8 to my thoughts every day.

"Finally, brothers, whatever is true, whatever is noble, whatever is right, whatever is pure, whatever is lovely, whatever is admirable—if anything is excellent or praiseworthy—think about such things."

Thank you, Judy, for allowing God to use you through *Feelings Women Rarely Share*. Thank you for helping to save my life. I was headed down a road of total destruction, and I finally feel free.

Unsigned

Introduction

"Judy," my friend Joan asked, "I understand you're writing a book. What's it about?"

"Lust," I replied.

"Lust? What lust? Excessive spending, eating? What lust?

"No, it's about sexual lust," I answered.

"Come on, Judy," Joan said. "What in the world would you know about that subject? Stop kidding me! Where would you have learned anything?"

I laughed and replied, "From my friends, Joan, from my friends."

I wrote this book not as an authority on the subject of lust but simply because it needed to be addressed. A surprising lack of information is available to Christian women on how to prevent becoming entangled in sexual temptation.

When friends began to confide in me about these problems in their own lives, I had no answers. So I packed my pen and legal pad in my briefcase and headed off to the library. After many hours of research, I found I was really being turned off by the permissiveness and perversion of ethics and anti Judeo-Christian teaching. The suggestions in these books bordered on soft pornography, and almost all gave license to sexual promiscuity.

My next trip was to the local Christian bookstore. There I found many excellent books on marriage, single living, family life, sex techniques, and parenting. Some of these are listed in the Suggested Reading section of this book. I did not, however, find a book dealing with the subject of lust in Christian women. So, "I milked many cows but churned my own butter." My best insight came from spending time alone with God and allowing Him to mold my thoughts.

Actual case histories, letters, and personal interviews with women willing to tell me their stories also provided valuable information. I appreciate all their help because I know they have shared with me *feelings women rarely share.*

But because many women have not shared these feelings with others, they have "missed the mark of the high calling of Christ." Unaware of how our emotions and our bodies respond in certain situations, Christian women are falling into a trap set by our enemy, Satan.

More than ever, Christian women must be taught, in complete honesty, about temptation and sexual lust. We can no longer afford to be deceived because many of us are on the way to becoming an "accident about to happen."

Recently I conducted a workshop in a mid-western city, and the topic of morality surfaced. We had been discussing how men and women, especially those whose ministry involves being away from their families often, must be wise in their dealings with the opposite sex. One woman reacted strongly. "I heard someone teach on lust recently. Now those who had attended that seminar talk openly about it. I'm so tired of hearing about sexual lust. I think it has become a fad," she said.

Teaching on lust must never become the "in" thing. It's a subject that needs to be addressed to every Christian woman, I hope, only once. I pray the market does not become flooded and our minds glutted with teachings on adultery.

My purpose in writing this book is to talk openly about a subject that is not readily taught in the Body of Christ—the problems of sexual lust in women

(Christian women) and how to prevent becoming involved in sexual sin. I believe that multitudes of married Christian women will experience, at least once in their lifetime, promiscuous feelings toward another man. When they do, I pray that this book will help them be prepared.

To my readers, I want you to know that my "complete portfolio" of knowledge and understanding on this subject at this time is written on these pages. If you need additional help after reading this book, please seek that counsel from a credible source such as your own pastor.

While I am aware that this book has been addressed primarily to married women, I realize that some readers may be single, widowed, or divorced. Many unmarried women have come up to me after a seminar on this subject and said, "I know that I can use so much of what I've learned. I'm glad I came."

Another woman said to me, "I have no idea why I came to hear you speak about lust in women." The next day this woman went to the beauty shop. While she was there, the beautician, who was her close friend, received a male visitor. Through the overtones and the body language, my friend realized something was going on that shouldn't be. After her appointment, my friend took out her notes and shared what she had learned at my seminar. The beautician received the correction and cut off her relationship with this other man.

Some of the topics women have asked me to include in the book center particularly on the marriage bed. But since my purpose was to zero in on the topic of lust, many of the side issues had to be excluded. Other authors who have specifically addressed these issues are at the end of this book in the Suggested Reading List. Also, in my six tape series (9 hours), "An Honest Look at Marital Sex," I cover the subject very frankly. The album is $35. You may send a check to Judy Reamer, P.O. Box 500606, Atlanta, GA 31150.

You may not enjoy what you read in the following pages. *Learning warfare strategy is not enjoyable.* But it is impossible to resist the enemy until we know his battle plans. The time has come to learn how to discern, resist, and conquer. "Affair prevention" is what this book is all about.

With that in mind, I offer this book in love.

1

Tempted? Who, Me?

> "We are half-hearted creatures fooling about with drink and sex and ambition when Infinite joy is offered us, like an ignorant child who wants to go on making mud pies in a slum because he cannot imagine what is meant by the offer of a holiday at the sea. We are far too easily pleased."—C. S. Lewis[1]

A young pastor of a small congregation had little experience in counseling with women. So, unable to refer to case histories, he asked his wife, "Honey, do women ever get tempted with sexual feelings?"

She answered, "Oh, yes, of course."

Her husband said, "Have you ever been tempted, honey?"

"Oh, yes," she replied.

"Will you tell me who it was?"

"Oh, no!" she said.

Yes, there are some feelings women rarely share. In fact, until recently, I do not recall hearing any of these confidences over the years: "Judy, I've got a problem. I can't stop thinking about this guy even though he's married"; or, "Judy, I had a sexual dream last night, and it involved so and so."

Females characteristically enjoy maintaining privacy. You've probably heard the old saying: Two things unknown about a person are how much money he has in the bank and what goes on in his bedroom. As Christians, we have no need to hide our bank accounts. Why would we? But what goes on in our bedroom is sacred, private, and intimate, and we *do* want to keep that a secret.

When a Christian woman has been tempted, she becomes highly secretive about what's going on inside her. Several reasons may warrant her secrecy. First, she may believe that only men have a problem with lust-filled thoughts. Or, she may believe that if women do have sexual thoughts, surely *Christian* women do not have these temptations.

A second reason for her secrecy may be that if a woman has grown in her spiritual walk, she *knows* what God's Word says about sexual sin and may repress her thoughts or feel guilty because of it, as in, thou shall not *admit* adultery.

But among you there must not be even a hint of sexual immorality, or of any kind of impurity, or of greed, because these are improper for God's holy people. Nor should there be obscenity, foolish talk or coarse joking, which are out of place, but rather thanksgiving. For of this you can be sure: No immoral, impure or greedy person—such a man is an idolater—has any inheritance in the kingdom of Christ and of God. Let no one deceive you with empty words, for because of such things God's wrath comes on those who are disobedient (Ephesians 5:3–7, *NASB*).

Surprise or shock over her own lustful feelings may also keep a woman enveloped in secrecy. One woman said, "I recognized all the symptoms as part of my unsaved life. What startled me was that these were now showing up in my Christian walk." These emotions may bring *sweet pleasure* to her, so she puts them on *simmer* rather than on *off.*

Therefore, instead of admitting or confessing that she is being tempted, a Christian woman will suppress rather than express her feelings. Unfortunately, suppression delays her from seeking early counsel and allows even further problems to develop.

A Secret No More

Are women really having problems with lust? A well-known women's magazine recently asked readers to complete a questionnaire on intimate experiences. Ninety-three percent of those responding indicated a belief in God. Tucked in among the questions on marriage, childbearing, and self-esteem was this one: Have you ever been tempted to have an affair? Forty-seven percent of the women indicated they had been tempted. That's an incredible amount, considering some of their answers to other questions. Thirty-nine percent said they had problems with moodiness, and thirty-four percent said they had experienced depression.

According to this survey, women are having more problems with sexual temptation than with moodiness or depression. Isn't that a surprising statistic?

The way the Lord got my attention on this subject came during a three-month period. During that time, I was bombarded with stories from women whom I would never have dreamed were having problems with lust. These stories were told to me *in confidence,* so I could not share the prayer burden with anyone.

The stories kept coming and coming until I felt completely overwhelmed.

I thought, "Why is all this happening?"

I looked forward to a long ministry trip in a city far from my home. Oh, was I glad to get away from the weight of the women's needs! (Oh, if only the weight had been in pounds . . .) But while I was away, two pastor's wives came to me on separate occasions and shared what was happening in their lives regarding sexual temptation. I could not get away from what I felt was becoming an epidemic.

When I returned home, I met with a man who worked as a counselor with an evangelistic ministry. He said, "Judy, I agree that there must be an epidemic because most of the people that I counsel are having problems in the sexual area."

"Oh, God," I asked, "why are You allowing me to see this all now?"

Then clearly I felt He was saying to me, "I'm prodding you to speak out on this subject."

I felt as Balaam must have in Numbers 22:20, when God said, "But yet the word which I say unto thee, that shalt thou do." I, like Balaam, seemed to have "no way to turn either to the right hand or to the left" (verse 26). God had definitely "walled me in" to speak about something that was grieving His heart.

Then I began to question pastors about this message. "Is this really needed?" I repeatedly asked. "Can this be of God?" "Are women coming to you with these problems?" Each one of my questions was answered without hesitation—yes, yes, yes.

It seems as though men know more about us women in this area than we do ourselves; because, when a woman finally goes for counseling, she usually goes to her pastor. Therefore, male pastors and counselors have learned about the torments while women remain unknowledgeable regarding the frequency of this problem. Temptation is "common to man," (1 Corinthians 10:13, *NIV*) and that includes women also.

Since I have begun to teach on this subject of sexual lust, I have heard some incredible stories from married women. No one seems immune. Young and old, rich and poor, happily married and unhappily married have shared with me their struggle with sexual lust. We should not be shocked or surprised when it occurs.

"My brethren, count it all joy *when* ye fall into divers temptations; knowing this, that the trying of your faith worketh patience" (James 1:2–3, *italics added*). Scripture does not say *if* temptation comes but *when* temptation comes.

In regard to sexual temptation, I want to clarify that these are *not* tests from God. In *Vine's Expository Dictionary*, W. E. Vine clearly expresses my own thoughts. He says, "But though such temptation does not proceed from God, yet does God regard His people while they endure it, and by it tests and approves them."

When temptation comes, we need to know how to get help. James tells us that while we are in the midst of temptation, we can call upon God for wisdom. "If any of you lack wisdom, let him ask of God, that giveth to all men liberally, and upbraideth not; and it shall be given him" (James 1:5).

Why Do We Need Wisdom?

The first reason I needed God's wisdom about this problem was because I wanted protection for myself. "Physician, heal thyself," Luke 4:23 says. I wanted understanding in *my* life and in *my* situations. I did not want to become one of the statistics of an adulterous affair. "Tempted? Who, me?" I asked the Lord. "Yes, Judy," came His response, "you need these weapons because of the nature of a traveling ministry."

The second reason I needed wisdom was to help others find protection and/or freedom from a sinful situation. Wouldn't it be a terrible thing if American lives were suddenly endangered by a possible nuclear accident, and we were not told of the impending danger? Those who are secretly in shame or shock over a tempting situation need to be assured that they are not alone. The Lord can and will set the captive free. "Because he himself suffered when he was tempted, he is able to help those who are being tempted" (Hebrews 2:18, *NIV*).

Many times after I have spoken on this subject, women have come to me and said, "I wondered why I was here. Surely, I thought, this message could not be for me. But I'm glad I came. I really needed to hear it." An ounce of prevention is worth a pound of cure.

Perhaps some of you have picked up this book out of curiosity and feel this message is not for you either. But God's Word tells us, "Be sober, be vigilant; because your adversary the devil, as a roaring lion, walketh about, seeking whom he may devour" (1 Peter 5:8).

I would much rather concentrate on *preventing* an affair than on helping someone disentangle herself from one.

Lastly, we women need to have wisdom regarding our physical bodies and how to control our urges and desires:

> It is God's will that you should be holy; that you should avoid sexual immorality; that each of you should learn to control his own body in a way that is holy and honorable, not in passionate lust like the heathen, who do not know God . . . For God did not call us to be impure, but to live a holy life (1 Thessalonians 4:3–5,7, *NIV*).

Each of us is a unique creation of God. Your biological make-up is different from mine. That is why each of us needs to know *herself.* The above scriptures are talking about control—not in the sense of being domineering and manipulative toward others but rather control as it relates to our sexual drives.

None of us is above temptation. Charlie Shedd said in his book, *Letters To Philip: How To Treat A Woman,* that the "temptation to infidelity is not a rare occurrence but standard equipment on some of the best models."

In this sex-saturated society, God is calling women to holiness. I fully realize that this is a tough assignment when we live in such a jungle of sexual bombardments—but not impossible with God's help. In the following chapters, you will learn how to recognize some of God's warning signals and how to prevent a sinful situation from ever getting off the ground.

Oops!

Let me tell you how I overreacted in one incident.

Years ago my husband Bernie and I invited a couple—new to our church—to our home. Being an architect, Ron began walking around the rooms looking at the design of our house. Bernie and Dolores, Ron's wife, had wandered off to look at the kitchen. I thought this man was shy; but as soon as Bernie was out of the room, he stopped in the middle of the living room, looked me right in the eye, and said, "Judy, I really do like your chest."

My mind began to spin, and I reached out for an answer to match my charming facade. What nerve, I thought. How could this be happening? Where's Bernie when I need him? But good old Judy, sometimes an A student in bloopers, did it again. I said, in order to diffuse his freshness, "Thank you, I really like your chest, too."

This artistic man, who knew every color on the palate, proceeded to turn them all at once. I thought both of us would sink into the carpet.

"Ah, um, I meant, I really like your buffet—whatever that piece of teak furniture is over there," he finally answered.

"Oh, dear," I said. "I thought the demon of lust was staring me right in the face, and my answer to you was one of sheer horror!"

We laughed with gusto—not lusto.

Wouldn't it be great if all potentially lustful situations would wind up as innocuous and light-hearted as that one?

Unfortunately, they don't. But when the real situations surface, we must, with God's help, know how to prevent a sinful situation from occurring and how to "abstain from all appearance of evil" (I Thessalonians 5:22).

I pray that you will not acquire a "lust mentality" from reading this book. For a while the subject of lust may be emphasized in your mind, but don't go looking for it in others or jump to the wrong conclusions.

After reading this book, I hope you will never be naive or deceived again. As these pages linger in your mind, may the Holy Spirit bring you to the places in the book that need to be considered in your own life. Reread those places and open up to God.

Putting these principles into practice in your own life could save you costly mistakes. One of the most costly mistakes ever made by a large automobile manufacturer was a recall of 4.9 million cars to check for faulty carburetors and exhaust systems. The postage alone cost more than four million dollars for the registered letters sent to the buyers.

This book is written to be a check for our "carburetors and exhaust systems" so that God may send us out with no costly mistakes. The cost to His Kingdom involves much more than money.

Near Sacramento, California, detectors alerting freeway drivers that they have made an incorrect turn are sometimes buried in the pavement. A loud horn sounds, and a twelve-inch red light illuminates a sign that reads, "Go back. You're going the wrong way!" The loud warnings sounded throughout this book are meant to be your "lust busters."

"Who, me—a wrong way driver? Never." "Who, me—tempted?" we say as we giggle uncomfortably.

I pray you will keep reading, for you are precious jewels in God's Kingdom—too precious to be part of what is abominable to God.

2

Drives, Desires, and Decisions

"If I find in myself desires which nothing in this world can satisfy, the only logical explanation is that I was made for another world."—C. S. Lewis[1]

Sex should not make the world go around. But it sure has sent some people spinning right off their axis because of its power.

Sexual thoughts permeate our lives. Television programs, magazine articles, and advertising campaigns, all remind us that we are sexual beings. Shampoo, toothpaste, and deodorant have become sexual status symbols. Whether we are aware of them or not, subliminal messages about sex are all around us.

Current advertising strategy, however, has become anything but subliminal. Teenagers are being told to "Just say no" to sex, but this is far from the message they are receiving. From food to clothes to perfumes our living rooms are bombarded in prime time viewing exhorting that sex is fun, safe, and loving.

These deceptive messages from blatant advertising campaigns send out the message that if it feels good—do it. They imply that to live without sexual expression is unreasonable and unbearable even if it means taking the risk of contracting a deadly disease. "You are entitled to have what you want, and you should not repress what you want," say the ads.

One female rock star was asked this question on a daytime TV talk show. "I understand," the interviewer said, "that the other female members of your group say the group broke up mainly because of your sexual involvement with their guys. Is that correct?"

"Well," she replied, "I'm not sure if that's the reason, but I have had sex with their guys. Why shouldn't I? When I see something I want, I go after it."

Thank the Lord most of us are not that aggressive or sinful about our needs. In fact, most women are reluctant to talk about their sexual needs. A unique characteristic of Christian women is that they delay going for help longer. They're more secretive.

I well remember the first time I was called to speak at a seminar about intimacy in the marriage relationship. I felt so uncomfortable even mentioning the word *sex* that I started my message by saying, "This afternoon we are going to talk about. . . . Then I paused and spelled out the word S . . . um . . . E . . . um . . . X." The response to the message was amazing, and I left that seminar in a daze. I could not get over how many other women were also spellers and really needed to get beyond their shyness to talk about their problems in this area.

Sex Is God's Idea

God ordained marriage so that we could know one person intimately. The marital relationship is a *type* of relationship to God. Christ refers to Himself as the bridegroom and the Church as his bride. (See John 3:29.) All through Paul's writings he compares the human marriage relationship to the oneness we share with Christ in our heavenly marriage.

Dr. Francis Schaeffer said, "My personal opinion is that the marriage relationship is not just an illustration, but rather that in all things—including the marriage relationship—God's external creation speaks of Himself."

The marital relationship is also described in scripture as a *mystery:*

> For this cause shall a man leave his father and mother, and shall be joined unto his wife, and they two shall be one flesh. This is a great *mystery;* but I speak concerning Christ and the church (Ephesians 5:31–32, *italics added*).

Once I heard a pastor say that he thought this passage would have sounded more spiritual if God had said one *spirit.* But He didn't. He said *flesh.* One flesh. Cleaving to one flesh excludes marital unfaithfulness.

What does becoming *one flesh* mean in God's eyes? God sees the physical act of becoming one in the flesh as more than having sexual intercourse. Becoming one flesh with another individual means, in God's sight, that our triune—body, soul, and spirit—has also become involved in this union. It is impossible to divide or separate us in our totality. Not even a surgeon's scalpel can separate what God has created.

God blesses sex only within marriage. That is why *satisfying* sex can only be found within those boundaries. Physically satisfying maybe, but not worth the trade-off that carries with it guilt, condemnation, and, usually, the death of that relationship.

A sexual relationship between two people not married to each other will soon cause the entire relationship to lose its value. One man said, "Having an affair would be like using my Cadillac as though it were a pickup truck."

Ah, if only the following were the testimony of every spouse:

> A boy heard a safe sex message in school. He came home and asked his grandfather, "How did you practice safe sex?" "I wore a wedding ring."

Our Internal Motivators

Within each of us, God created certain biological needs or drives that motivate our lives. These needs must be met to satisfy that pulsating inner drive. The primary needs are hunger, thirst, sleep, and sex. "When such primary needs are not met, a primary drive builds up within one's body, motivating the individual to satisfy that need."[2]

How those primary needs are met, however, differs. Without food or water we would die. Because we would also die without sleep, God made our bodies to shut off automatically until that sleep need is satisfied.

But here is the big shock: *You will not die without sex.*

Even though our social messages imply that you will die—you won't. The sex drive is the one motivating drive that the body can live without.

A common thread of deception that runs through the "I'm having an affair" story is similar to this one.

"Judy," a woman told me, "I absolutely cannot live without him."

My next question was, "Okay, why do you think you can't live without him?"

"Because," she said, "he makes me feel special."

Each time I have asked that question, the answer has had nothing to do with sexual intercourse. Instead, the relationship has met the woman's need for *intimacy and uniqueness,* and sexual intercourse has *not* been the primary need.

Dr. Ed Cole explained why a husband should minister to a woman's uniqueness.

Every woman needs to know she is unique to her man. That's why even women who are promiscuous feel a measure of guilt in having sexual relations without any love. So, prior to submitting to a man's love-making, they ask the age old question, "Do you love me?" Mechanical sex cannot satisfy the desire for true intimacy. You assure your wife of your love for her when you tell her she is the one God wanted you to have.[3]

If a woman does not feel unique in the male/female relationship, she suffers from loneliness; and in her loneliness, she often begins her search for intimacy with another person.

In Search of Intimacy

Intimacy and sexual intercourse are not synonymous, as many believe. Intimacy involves openness, dropping defenses, caring and sharing, surrendering control, and a host of other warm, human traits. What is interesting is that while studies show both males and females need intimacy, the male is almost totally unaware of this need or the ability to create such a relationship.

Women, however, are very aware of their need for intimacy. Some mistakenly believe, though, that marriage is the cure-all for loneliness, boredom, or lack of self-fulfillment.

One columnist wrote, "Real loneliness consists not in being alone, but in being with someone in the suffocating darkness of a room in which no deep communication is possible."

Our need for intimacy involves the whole person—body, soul, and spirit.

Let's look first at our *spiritual* need for intimacy. Within each of us, God placed a vacuum—a special place, which only He Himself can fill. Until that vacuum has been filled with His presence, men and women go on searching, often trying to fill that gap with worldly things.

G.K. Chesterton said, "Every man who knocks on the door of a brothel is looking for God."

However, as Oswald Chambers writes, "There is only One being who can satisfy the last aching abyss of the human heart, and that is the Lord Jesus Christ."

Often while we are searching to fill that special place, we look to the most unlikely sources. Our search is for a situation or location that is transcendent, a word which connotes excellence. Something that is *separate from* or *beyond* experience or the material universe. Like a story that is beyond belief, superior to any other. I experienced it many times as a youngster. Here's why:

> As teens, my two best friends (Shelly and Ruthie) and I would climb to the $1.25 balcony seats at the Forest Theater (Philadelphia), where we would watch the pre-Broadway tryouts of all the musicals

heading for New York. The trip there was anything but transcendent as I recall moving from bitter cold winds into the warm theater after a *long* subway ride, which was preceded by a *long* bus ride, which was preceded by a *long* three-block trek to the bus stop, which was preceded by an exit from my less than ideal home environment. Oh, but once we got there . . .

The 2 P.M. Saturday matinee would start with its melodic orchestral overture. The curtain ascended onto a larger-than-life musical comedy production. Eventually came signature songs like "Hello Dolly" (*Hello Dolly*), "Seventy-Six Trombones" (*The Music Man*), "Mame" (*Mame*), "If Ever I Should Leave You" (*Camelot*), "Ole Man River" (*Showboat*), or "On the Street Where You Live" (*My Fair Lady*).

Sitting in the dark with my heavy coat draped on my knees, I was emotionally moved by the *transcendent* beauty of the sets, the *transcendent* colorful costumes, the *transcendent* power of the musical comedy voices, and the *transcendent* harmony of the orchestra's instruments. This was so opposite of what represented life to me outside.

Broadway musicals were perfect! I was taken to a place in my young heart that caused it to overflow with joy. It was too much happiness for me. I couldn't bear it. Nothing else could take me to such heights of delight and peace in my soul like those shows of the 50s. They were out of this world. They were *transcendent*. I cried inside for I knew it was only make believe; it was going to end. In a way I was wishing the music and the actors weren't so perfectly wonderful. Because . . . when the curtain descended I would be back to the street for the bitter cold walk to the subway, then the transfer to the bus, then the three-block walk home, and back into . . . *not easy.*

The day will come when we'll leave this *not easy* home and enter a warm theater to be a part of a show that has music, costumes and scenery, melodic voices, and the Hero of all ages. If we are God's, we'll be able to climb up onto the stage and sing and dance and wear handsome garb and it will all be perfect. The curtain will never go down, the show will never end, and we shall never have to go out in the cold. We'll taste *transcendence* as a gut level reality. No tears in Heaven? Oh Lord, at least let us cry in thanksgiving!

Not many people have tasted transcendence through a Broadway musical because New York is just too far away. And, likewise, few believers are heavenly minded because it too seems too far away. Is it sometimes too difficult to imagine that we will be on the stage of the most successful production ever written? The signature song is "Amazing Grace." We never auditioned, we were not skilled, and we had no experience. We just don't deserve this, but none less than the Casting Director (our Father) has chosen us.

However, as it is written: "No eye has seen, no ear has heard, no mind has conceived what God has prepared for those who love him" (1 Corinthians 2:9, 10, *NIV*), but God has revealed it to us by his Spirit.

The desire for transcendence is descriptive of why multitudes have come to God. Did we primarily come to the Lord for relief and pleasure? Yes?

Why were we created? What is our purpose here on earth? Many mistakenly believe it is to find personal fulfillment and satisfaction. Likened to my going to a Broadway musical . . .

That is why when life got *not easy* down here, and it did, we went looking for lesser gods, looking for a new person to bring life to our disappointed flesh. But, if we came to God in sorrow because we saw we had sinned against Him, and therefore, were going to suffer forever, then when *not easy* occurred we didn't think of looking for a new god. We remembered that Jesus told us we would have troubles. We factored those into our lives down here. The Old Testament seems to have promised prosperity to the Jewish nation, but when I read my Bible it appears that the New Testament promises adversity to all the citizens on earth who belong to a heavenly kingdom. Our home as believers is not down here.

Yes, adversity, but we have gained acceptance by God through forgiveness, been made new in our identity, received the Holy Spirit as a resident inside, and can look with certainty to a heavenly eternity. There *are* promises to God's children in the New Testament which make our heart glad . . . but to deny the "trouble" parts will lead us to be confused, frustrated, and distrustful of what we have read is a good and loving God.

The prophet Jeremiah found the answer to why we were created. "Thus saith the Lord, Let not the wise man glory in his wisdom, neither let the mighty man glory in his might, let not the rich man glory in his riches: but let him that glorieth glory in this, that he understandeth and knoweth me" (Jeremiah 9:23).

Once each of us understands that our main purpose here in life is to know God—to have that intimate, personal, relationship with the King of the Universe—then all of life falls into its rightful place.

God wants to be known by us. He initiated the relationship. We did not choose Him; He first chose us. We could desire to have a relationship with the President of the United States to no avail, unless he first summoned us into his chamber. God did summon us. He called us into a lifelong, personal, intimate fellowship with the Godhead.

Now let me say something that may be the pivotal point of this entire book.

We are not the center of the universe.

God is. Our entire purpose for having a relationship with God is not to get Him to work on our behalf to fulfill our every want and need; but rather, we were created to please Him. My favorite verse in the Word is Rev. 4:11 because it keeps me mentally sober regarding how God has it all set up. Everything is for His pleasure . . .

"You are worthy, our Lord and God, to receive glory and honor and power, for you created all things, and by your will they were created and have their being" *(NIV)*.

Soulish Desires

King Solomon is a good example of one who saturated his life, fulfilling every soulish desire, whim, and fantasy. Exploring many avenues of occupation, Solomon became a master architect, administrator, diplomat, tradesman, and equestrian. His many hobbies ranged from geology and zoology to writing and gardening.

Solomon satiated his motivating drives with his philosophy that one should eat, drink, and be merry. (See Ecclesiastes 2:24.) "And he had seven hundred wives, princesses, and three hundred concubines" (1 Kings 11:3). Now that's a man who had no problem with temptation. Whenever it came his way, he gave into it. But the remaining passage tells us of his plight.

> For it came to pass, when Solomon was old, that his wives turned away his heart after other gods: and his heart was not perfect with the Lord his God. . . . And the Lord was angry with Solomon. . . . The Lord said unto Solomon, Forasmuch as this is done of thee, and thou hast not kept my covenant and my statutes, which I have commanded thee, I will surely rend the kingdom from thee (1 Kings 11:4, 9, 11).

I have spoken with women whose experiences were similar to Solomon's. They've told me what heartache has come into their lives as their families were torn apart because they decided to fulfill a selfish, soulish desire. Broken homes, broken lives, and broken hearts are the results of satisfied lust.

As Solomon scanned his life for a meaningful conclusion, he left this message for his sons: You do not have to submit to your every soulish desire.

> Rejoice, O young man, in thy youth; and let thy heart cheer thee in the days of thy youth, and walk in the ways of thine heart, and in the sight of thine eyes; but know thou, that for all these things God will bring thee into judgment. Therefore, remove sorrow from thy heart, and put away evil from thy flesh (Ecclesiastes 11:9–10).

Solomon was right in his observation, "There is nothing new under the sun." Men and women still seek to please themselves before they count the cost. As Solomon contemplated his eventual death, his final words ring down through the pages of time instructing us, also.

> Let us hear the conclusion of the whole matter: Fear God, and keep his commandments: for this *is* the whole *duty* of man. For God shall bring every work into judgment, with every secret thing, whether *it be* good, or whether it *be* evil (Ecclesiastes 12:13–14).

Sexual Needs

Before I became a believer, I lived entirely in the body and soul realm of existence. I wasn't aware that I had a spirit. But when I became aware that my dead spirit had become alive in Christ, I made up my mind to ignore my physical realm. How could my bodily needs bring glory to a spiritual God? I thought.

For several weeks I avoided Bernie by falling asleep before he did, or I invented projects to stay up later than he did. Bernie was not yet a believer and could not have understood my spiritual decision to remain chaste. How pure I felt—lonely—but pure.

Soon after having made this decision, I heard about a large Christian convention in Washington, D.C., that I wanted to attend. Bernie, who was not yet a believer, agreed to go with me. We met some dear friends of ours at the convention and enjoyed the fellowship and banquet.

I was all prepared to hear this dynamic speaker give us a special word that would change us more into the image and character of our Lord.

It was a special word all right! But my interpretation of it would have more than changed our lives. It would have destroyed our marriage.

The evangelist spoke on total commitment, tying in the subject of eunuchs in the Bible as a type of total dedication. I became very excited when I heard what he was going to talk about since I had just made the decision to forego my own sex life. I thought the speaker implied that if we really wanted to serve God, we should assume, literally, the cessation of sex, as if we, too, had been "castrated."

When it came time for the altar call, the evangelist asked all who wanted to be eunuchs for the Lord to stand at their seats and declare so publicly. I stood immediately, thinking I was making a commitment to God to remain celibate the rest of my life. Poor Bernie, who had no idea what was going on, remained seated.

What a glorious and awesome commitment I had made, I thought. I looked around, and my friends at our table had also stood. They, too, had heeded the call to celibacy. We could stand together. Sex was for the worldly. I liked sex—I liked it a lot. But now I had given it up to please my God.

After the meeting was over, we three women found our way to my hotel room for a chance to talk. When the door was shut behind us, I rejoiced loudly with them about how we had just given up our sexuality to become eunuchs for the Lord. Their faces went blank.

"What do you mean, Judy?" one of the women asked. "Surely you don't think the speaker asked us to give up having sex. You're kidding, aren't you?"

"No, I'm serious," I replied.

"Oh, Judy," the other friend said, "that can't be. I enjoy lovemaking with my husband. I did not stand up to lay that down."

The two of them continued to assure me that what the speaker really meant was that we were to surrender all of ourselves to God in a total commitment. Sexual intercourse is God's plan for marriage—and not to be denied.

I smiled wanly and felt horribly stupid and embarrassed.

God used that situation, however, to send me straight to the Bible to bury myself in study about the subject of sexuality. What a change occurred in my life! God saved me from my "eunuch fever," gave me solid instruction in the Word, and increased my pleasure with my husband.

Thank God my friends interpreted correctly what the Spirit of God was trying to convey that night. If I had gone on to teach my error, church growth would have plummeted to zero population.

Exactly what does sexuality have to do with spirituality? Louis McBurney said it well:

There is a similarity between spirituality and sexuality. In both, we lower personal barriers, encourage intimacy, become open and vulnerable and experience profoundly moving emotions. Some individuals compare their deepest spiritual moments to a sexual climax. Both provide an intense response, a loss of ego boundaries, and a sense of oneness with the one who shares the experience.[4]

God does have a purpose for physical expression in marriage. Tim and Beverly LaHaye write,

Behind their closed bedroom door, a couple experiences oneness—a sublime moment uniting them in an exclusively intimate union unshared by anyone else on earth. That is the major reason why the act of marriage is such a binding, uniting, and enriching influence on a couple.[5]

Dealing with Unmet Needs

What about the women, however, who are involved in a marriage relationship where the needs for sexual fulfillment and/or intimacy are unmet?

You only need to walk into a bookstore or speak with any counselor to know how great that need is. Illness and physical disabilities may prevent sexual expression. Mental or emotional disturbances may also affect a couple's level of intimacy.

One young woman wrote telling me that because of her husband's disability, sexual intercourse could never be experienced again. Another wrote about a husband who never wants sex unless she asks for it, and this was humiliating to her. Still another wrote explaining of her frustration with a husband who failed to understand both her physical and her emotional needs.

All too often this is when the imagination takes over and the "forbidden fruit" begins to look mighty good. Unless a woman has dealt with those desires to experience the forbidden *before marriage,* she probably will not put forth the effort to search for a godly solution if she encounters marital problems. Instead, she may continue to center on her own selfish needs, which will eventually lead to sin.

Michael Cavanaugh calls this "the taste for stolen water."

> Have you developed a taste for stolen water? Does the idea of taking something forbidden attract you? Many people think that once they get married their desire for the forbidden will go away. They believe their struggles against sexual sin should end because they can now have sex righteously within marriage. But that's not what happens. Because the righteous relationship of marriage does not satisfy the person's taste for the forbidden, they're left struggling with the same temptations as before. . . . That's why your struggles with sexual sin aren't going to go away the minute you get married. That's why you'll still be tempted to the lure of pornography—movies, magazines, and books—and illicit sex. That's why you'll struggle with unfaithfulness even though you really love your spouse. You've got a taste for stolen waters.[6]

The way to deal with unmet needs, then, is to make yourself fully aware that fulfilling your every desire is not God's ultimate plan.

I was in the audience when Elizabeth Elliott, a renowned author, answered this question of a single woman.

"As I am unmarried, wouldn't God remove my desire for physical intimacy if it couldn't be fulfilled?"

"Not necessarily," she offered. *"He's scouring your very foundations.* He's wanting you to cry out to Him, to trust Him." Then she read Deuteronomy 8:1–3(*NIV*):

Be careful to follow every command I am giving you today, so that you may live and increase and may enter and possess the land that the LORD promised on oath to your forefathers. Remember how the LORD your God led you all the way in the desert these forty years, to humble you and to test you in order to know what was in your heart, whether or not you would keep his commands. *He humbled you, causing you to hunger and then feeding you with manna, which neither you nor your fathers had known, to teach you that man does not live on bread alone but on every word that comes from the mouth of the LORD (italics added).*

God's ultimate desire is that *Jesus Christ becomes your LORD.*

He wants you to lay down your life, your rights, and your needs so His will and purpose can be worked out through you.

In one instance, a woman's husband actually gave her permission to have a sexual relationship with another man because of his own disability. The answer is still NO WAY! God does not give that kind of permission. That husband could still satisfy the intimacy needs of his wife through his words, in gentle touching, and through adoration and sharing. Even though this woman was no longer able to find her fulfillment through a sexual expression, she could depend on God to turn her attention toward the other positive qualities in their relationship.

A woman's relationship with God is more valuable than any earthly relationship. The Bible tells us that we are to die to self-centeredness and to lay down our fleshly desires to glorify Him. Choosing to have an extramarital relationship is nothing more than placing yourself on God's throne.

There simply is no justification for sex outside of marriage!

Having, therefore, built this foundation that you will not die without having sex, you can call on God and your inner resources for creative outlets. Let's go on now to discuss how Satan works to lead us astray.

3

Satan's Plot

"You can't keep the birds from flying over your head, but you can keep them from making a nest in your hair"—Martin Luther

Recently I asked one of my closest friends to email me briefly her tale of, "I'm a Survivor of Infatuation!" She and I were using millions of words with one another re: our simultaneous bouts with lusting after the wrong fellows *a.k.a.* "The Drawing Away"! We'd cry, yell aloud, laugh, email, preach, encourage and moan together. We've both learned *humongous* truths as she battled as a divorcée and I as a widow. (See the prologue at the start of this book.) Here's her email to me this morning:

I have thought about this so many times and this is what I believe to be true. My understanding may increase with time but, for now, here's what I see . . .

I was caught up in an emotional relationship that I knew was not God's will from the beginning, but it met a deep need in me (or so I thought) for affection and companionship. I bargained with God over and over to keep myself from completely falling apart. I finally had to face that no matter what I said or did, this person was not a God person and was never going to be a part of God's plan for my life. I had broken the relationship off many times in a two-year period because I feared God's displeasure. During this rebellion, I missed the intimacy I had known with the Lord, but I would always go back to this man. I had never really faced the truth about my lack of trust in God and the deep emptiness inside, which only God could fill. I finally did face these things and I was so heartsick for the presence of the Lord that I broke the "bond" completely.

Unless I had been truly born again and had had a vital (life giving) relationship with God in the past, I would not have missed His presence when it was gone. (And it will be gone if we continue in disobedience.) I knew I could live without the feelings I was getting from this man (even though there were times when I felt I couldn't), but *I could not live without God's presence.* This drove me to end the relationship and begin again to seek the only one that will ever satisfy my deepest unmet needs.

I still have a ways to go—I still do not sense His presence like before, but I am trusting Him for that to return . . . if in His mercy He will favor me with that feeling again. If I never feel Him like I did before my disobedience, I will continue (by His grace) to seek and serve Him.

Some of you can relate to my dear friend above and you have *your* story. The plot is the same in every tale. An adversary ardently wants to get the distance between God and His children to be as far as the east is from the west.

Several years ago I listened to Jim Darnell, a good friend and an evangelist, deliver a message I have never forgotten. As I began to research the material for this book, my mind went back to that sermon, and I saw clearly how adultery and idolatry are closely linked.

I pray the Holy Spirit will let you see the awesomeness of Satan's plan—a conspiracy—to separate us from God and to draw our affections away from Him.

Let's look back at the scriptures to see how Satan planned to destroy God's people long ago. Today that plan is still in effect.

> While Israel was staying in Shittim, the men began to indulge in sexual immorality with Moabite women, who invited them to the sacrifices to their gods. The people ate and bowed down before these gods. So Israel joined in worshiping the Baal of Peor. And the Lord's anger burned against them (Numbers 25:1–3, *NIV*).

This passage tells us that because of sexual immorality, which led to idolatry, the Israelite people were drawn away from the true and living God. The end result was that God's wrath fell upon His people. Twenty-three thousand Israelites died from a mysterious plague, and one thousand more were hanged. Why did they experience such massive destruction? God's Word tells us it was because they set their hearts on evil things. First came sexual immorality, and then came idolatry.

Dr. Ed Cole says idolatry occurs when "you create something in your value system that has more worth to you than your devotion to God."

Every time I reread how Israel allowed Satan to deceive them, I feel angry. The Israelites valued their sensual pleasure rather than obedience to God's

Word. Yet it has happened over and over again, all the way up to this present age. Any time God's people fool around with "foreigners" (those who are off-limits because of marriage), they are asking for and will receive the label of idolater. As strange as the combination of pickles and ice cream is to the non-pregnant, so the combination of immorality and idolatry may appear to those without ears to hear what God is saying.

Jehovah God is a "jealous God" (Deuteronomy 5:9). His jealousy takes root in the fact that we may turn our backs on Him and be lost to intimacy with Him. He judged harshly as an example to the rest of His flock.

God told Moses to kill the leaders and expose the Israelites to the Lord's fierce anger. But while the whole scene of death and destruction was going on, one lust-filled "Israelite man (Zimri) brought to his family a Midianite woman right before the eyes of Moses and the whole assembly of Israel while they were weeping at the entrance to the Tent of Meeting." Apparently, the wrath of God did not mean anything to this man. I pray the end results of this couple's action will remain etched in our minds. "Phinehas . . . took a spear in his hand and . . . followed the Israelite into the tent. He drove the spear through both of them—through the Israelite and into the woman's body" (Numbers 25:6–7, NIV). The following sentence in verse eight is the most important one. "Then the plague against the Israelites was stopped."

God's judgment occurs when we entertain immorality. Break up the party, and God takes His judgment home. Phinehas ended the sinful situation without hesitation, discussion, or analysis. "Pluck out" the lust, and God will "pluck out" the plague.

Women who choose "to enter the tent" with Zimri will suffer the consequences of their choice.

Good understanding giveth favour: but the way of transgressors is hard (Prov. 13:15).

But among you there must not be even a hint of sexual immorality, or of any kind of impurity, or of greed, because these are improper for God's holy people. . . . Let no one deceive you with empty words, for because of such things God's wrath comes on those who are disobedient (Ephesians 5:3,6, *NIV*).

In the book, *Family Life: God's View of Relationships,* by Ray Stedman, is an explanation of how God's judgments work today.

The wrath of God, in this context (sex outside of marriage), is not a lightning bolt from heaven. It is not some fearsome catastrophe; some judgment that falls suddenly without warning—an auto accident or some terrible sickness—it is not that. The wrath of God is the invisible, almost imperceptible, but irresistible deterioration of life, the brutalizing of humanity, the vulgarizing of life. The reason we are suffering from this terrible tempest of neurosis and psychosis and mental anguish today is that we have disregarded these restrictions.[1]

One only needs to look at the social conditions today to know the full truth of those words. Unless a person repents, sexual immorality will eventually bring God's anger upon his life. And when God's anger falls, a family or an entire nation may feel the effect.

Why would sexual immorality cause the judgment of God to fall on a nation? Because the hearts of God's own people were turned away from Him by their own selfish, sexual lusts, and they worshipped the gods of their adulterous relationships. Satan plotted against God's people in order to separate them from God. The entire Old Testament is a history of how

Satan tried to corrupt the seed through which the Messiah passed.

And the Plot Goes On

Is it too far-out to think that for many recent decades Satan had a plot going on to do the very same thing in the United States?

Satan hates this nation. Ninety percent of all the missionaries sent throughout the world come from the United States. This nation was conceived in liberty, and its foundation was built on the Word of God.

Satan has quite a selection of plots, and the one presented here involves immorality. His plot is a horrible subject to talk about, but it is true.

This nation reminds me of the story of the frog who was placed in water and the heat turned up so gradually that by the time he realized he was being boiled to death, he was already half cooked.

In the past pornography was not allowed in the former Soviet Union. They did not allow sexual innuendoes on television, in movies and plays, or in books. Because the Soviets knew that *moral decay would destroy a country,* they used imprisonment as punishment for an off-color deed. Yet the very country that forbade pornography among their own people had many subversive KGB agents working through our media, through our congress, and through our newspapers influencing and giving much money to this cause.

Tomas Schuman, a defector who was once high up in the KGB, has said that eighty-five percent of their work was not James Bond stuff. Rather, it was subversive—a system that works secretly within the country. This former KGB agent said the first thing taught to an agent was how to demoralize a free country. It takes fifteen to twenty years to bring up one generation exposed to immorality. To do this, they brought in pornography, hard rock, and TV smut.

Multimedia programs have become increasingly vile and immoral. Television programs help establish the moral code of this country and also reflect it. Had we rejected the blatant sex and violence in the beginning, I do not believe the industry would keep pushing to see just how far they could go. The plot also controls the movie industry; and many magazines that were once respectable family reading now border on pornography.

When the former Soviet leader Yuri Andropov was alive, he told the communists that the USSR had practically accomplished the de-moralization of the USA. Years ago, Lenin foretold of this plan. It seems the plan has now been consummated.

That is what happened in America. Faithless people are now worshipping sex and perversion—all, that is, except for the remnant who remain true to the living God.

The Ultimate Goal

Now let's talk about the end results of immorality.

Satan's plan doesn't end in making us only immoral. The Moabite women got the Israelites involved in immorality for a reason. It was so they would be yoked to Baal. That is Satan's ultimate intention in immorality. That is the ramification of our flirtatiousness, of our fantasizing and daydreams, and of our sexual imaginings.

Yes, Satan tries to get you sidetracked from God's perfect will for your life, but that is not his ultimate intention. His intention is to see you cut off from communication with the true and living God. Those involved in immorality will inevitably experience this terrible predicament. Heaven will be as brass.

On Mt. Sinai, God gave Moses a commandment to tell His people. "Thou shalt not commit adultery." God knows all the reasons. He did not give this commandment to keep us from having fun but to keep us from experiencing spiritual death!

When we have allowed ourselves to be lured away from Father God, judgment awaits us. When God's people, the nation of Israel, indulged in sexual immorality, which turned them to idolatry, "the Lord's anger burned against them" (Numbers 25:3, *NIV*). This anger burned so hot that 24,000 Israelites died because of it.

Just read some of the stories the Holy Spirit of God recorded for us so that we might remember the cost of disobedience. Boils plagued the Egyptians, a bubonic-type plague devastated the Philistines, leprosy struck King Uzziah, leprosy came to Jeroboam, and a bowel disease came to Jehoram because of disobedience.

The apostle Paul said,

These things happened to them as examples and were written down as warnings for us, on whom the fulfillment of the ages has come. So, if you think you are standing firm, be careful that you don't fall (1 Corinthians 10:11–12, *NIV*).

An Angel of Light

Satan loves to deceive believers. When a believer has allowed herself to come under the plan of deception, Satan can use immorality to break down her relationship with God. All too often the deception starts with an innocent involvement with an ungodly man, such as when a married female believer tries to win an unsaved man to the Lord. She may well be on the road marked "this way to hell." Being confident in her own perceived spiritual maturity rather than in

God, this woman may travel far down the road before she is rescued.

Perhaps you are reading this and saying to yourself that could never happen to me. Never, never, never.

Let me share with you an experience I had several years ago when we lived in Maryland. On hot summer days, I took my children to the community center to swim. One day while I was watching them swim, I heard someone speaking with a marvelous accent. I turned around and saw one of the most handsome men I had ever laid eyes on. I said to him, "Where are you from?"

"Israel," he replied.

"You are!" I said. "What are you doing in America?"

"Well," he said, "the Jewish community has brought me over here to watch over the youth who are coming under the evangelism of Christians."

I sat there for a moment in disbelief. I thought, "He's been sent here to protect the kids from people like me!"

"Do you know what?" I asked. "I'm one of those people you are being paid to protect the kids from. I'm a believer in Jesus Christ."

"Oh," he said, "why don't you tell me about it."

And so I began to tell him how I came to know the Lord as my personal Savior.

Now, before we go any further with this story, I want to say that I was one person who *knew* I would never have any problems with immoral thoughts. Never, never, never. I had a marvelous marriage, and I loved my husband dearly. Immorality could never happen to me! Never!

I had entered into this conversation with this man strictly on a casual basis. As I talked to him, I began to think, Oh, God, here is an Israeli Jew who is going to come to the Lord. Thank you, God, for sending him here that I may witness to him. Isn't this wonderful?

He suggested that the next time I brought the children swimming I visit him in his office to tell him more about this Jesus. And so I did.

When I went to his office, I sat across from him and began to give him my testimony. He stared intently at me. He "oohed" and "aahed" at the right time and responded in all the right ways. All the while I thought how wonderful this was.

Since I couldn't finish the story in one trip, I came back the next week. We talked and talked and talked.

I told my friends about this Israeli Jew, and they were all praying for him. Everyone, including my husband, also thought, "How wonderful."

Twice a week, as the children swam, we continued to meet in his upstairs office. He began to say things such as, "Judy, I've never met anyone like you in my entire life."

"Oh," I would say, "you've just never met anyone who had God's Spirit living within them."

One day, however, this man said something that stuck with me. He said, "Judy, you have the most beautiful blue eyes."

At the time, I ignored the remark and went right on talking about Jesus.

But before my next visit with him, I remembered his comment and found myself reaching for my blue blouse that made my eyes look even bluer. Normally, I wore no makeup to the pool, but this time I even put on blue eye shadow. I also wanted my hair to look nice. How subtly it all starts.

We met for weeks. He would ask me questions about my faith and my personal life. I had never met anyone who was so interested in me and who had so much charm.

Then, one day, he dropped the bomb. He told me that his marriage wasn't going very well. He said, "Judy, I think I could make you happier than any other man."

I still cannot believe today that I sat there taking this all in. This man was suggesting that I go to bed with him!

Now you would think I would have *run* out of that office. But instead I went home remembering the warmth in his voice and thinking about what he had said.

The next day I decided that I better talk this thing over with my Christian friend who had been praying for him. I called her and asked if she would please come over to my house.

"Could I tell you what this man has been saying to me?" I asked, as we settled in over a cup of coffee.

As soon as she heard it, she literally shouted, "CUT IT OFF!"

Three words. That's all. But as soon as she said it, I knew it was from God. Immediately I realized what was going on. How could I, a spiritual wife and mother who taught God's Word, be so deceived? I sat there for a while in unbelief. I felt as though I had been in a semi-coma for the last few months. Half of my world had been lived out through the love of my husband and the other half through the pleasant, illicit feelings with this man.

When my friend spoke those three words, I felt as though an electric impulse had surged through me, and I was jolted back to a recognition of godliness and reality. When my confidante left, I lay on the floor before God, sobbing and asking how I had allowed myself to get into this situation. Not even my husband had known my state of mind during this time. Deception is like that.

But God promised in His Word, "If we confess our sins, he is faithful and just to forgive us our sins, and to cleanse us from all unrighteousness" (1 John 1:9, *NIV*). After a time of confession and repentance, I received that forgiveness along with the restoration of joy in my relationship with God.

My last contact with that man was a proposal, suggested by my friend, to bring another Christian with me during the visit, but he refused. And the relationship ended immediately.

If I had not shared my experience with a spiritual friend, I shudder to think what would have happened.

God's Word tells us that "Satan himself masquerades as an angel of light" (2 Corinthians 11:14, *NIV*). It is not surprising, then, that his servants masquerade also. (See verse 15.)

I now believe that this marvelous, handsome, gentle man was an enemy agent sent to lure me away from my heavenly Father.

What Should Be Our Attitude?

Potiphar, an Egyptian officer of Pharaoh and the captain of the guard, bought Joseph from the Ishmaelites and took him into his home. Joseph, being faithful in all his household duties, was then made overseer over Potiphar's home. All that Joseph did within that home prospered because the Lord was with him. There came a day, however, when Potiphar's wife "cast her eyes upon Joseph; and she said, Lie with me" (Genesis 39:7).

Joseph's first reaction was, This is not of God, and I'm getting out of here. He said, "How then can I do this great wickedness, and sin against God?" (Genesis 39:9).

That is the attitude we need to have toward immorality.

Don't see how close you can get to the fire before you get burned. Don't turn on the TV to see how much you can watch until it gets too bad for you. Don't read sexually stimulating books to see what's going on in the rest of the world. And don't stay in a situation where you know you will inevitably have to make a decision regarding immorality.

God never changes His plan to supply good things to His flock, nor does Satan ever change his intention to defrock the flock. Seduction, enticement, allurement, and solicitation are all arrows in his quiver. Those arrows are aimed at our most vulnerable area—our sexuality. "Break down their morality," he orders his henchmen.

If we are thoroughly aware of this plot against us, we will not and cannot be led out of God's camp and into the enemy's tent for his callous, tortuous undertakings. First the enemy gives us justifiable reasons to engage in sin, and then after we are so engaged he pours shame and hopelessness upon us. "How could you do such a thing???" the accuser rants.

4

Understanding the Ways of Temptation

"Exposure of the body in a personal encounter is like the telling of one's deepest secret: afterwards there is no going back, no pretending that the secret is still one's own or that the other does not know. It is, in effect the very last step in human relations, and therefore never one to be taken lightly. It is not a step that establishes intimacy, but one which presupposes it."—Mike Mason[1]

Since God tells us that at some point in each of our lives we will be tempted, we should understand two primary things about temptation. First, it is not God who tempts us—*temptation originates within our hearts.* Next, we must understand the way temptation works in order not to enter into it.

Let no man [woman] say when he [she] is tempted, I am tempted of God: for God cannot be tempted with evil, neither tempteth he any man [woman]: But every man [woman] is tempted, when he [she] is drawn away of his [her] own lust, enticed. Then when lust hath conceived, it bringeth forth sin: and sin, when it is finished, bringeth forth death. Do not err, my beloved forth death. Do not err, my beloved brethren (James 1:13–16).

Neither can a woman say, "The devil made me do it." Satan will come in only *after* the door has been opened to him. In verse fourteen we are clearly told where lust and temptation originate. Neither men nor women can be tempted unless they have first been drawn away by their own lust. A woman must first examine her own inner desires to determine when *she* opened the door of her mind to receive evil suggestions.

God has created each of us with *normal* longings, yearnings, and sexual appetites. Those appetites can conceive sin only when they are hooked up with the tempter. When we allow the bait (fantasizing, flirting, etc.) to dangle, the Evil One will gladly catch onto it.

Before the temptation to lust after another becomes conceived in our heart, God tells us to turn and RUN. "Flee fornication" (1 Corinthians 6:18). Immediate action—flee! It is the only sin He says that of, other than to flee youthful lusts. God knows the incredible pull of sexual sin. If we decide not to flee, we have made a decision to disobey and have actively taken the first step toward sin.

Hooking up Our Hang Ups

Let's look first at the normal desire of thirst. Thirst is a built-in, God-given, motivating desire for water that is necessary for our survival. If our desire to quench that thirst stays within the normal boundaries for water, juice, etc., we don't even hear Satan speak tempting thoughts to our minds. But if those desires to quench our thirst also link up with a desire to escape from the pressures of this world, then we become aware of Satan's voice. He may use these words: "Aren't you thirsty? Why don't you quench your thirst with something that will make you feel good also? How about a double scotch on the rocks to help you relax?"

If we were to decide that we needed "something" to get us through the day, something that would bring happiness or peace outside of God, then Satan's voice becomes known to us through our weakest areas. But unless we have first *chosen* to desire something other than what God has said is normal and right, our vulnerability to conceiving lust will be practically nil.

Sexual desire is every bit as strong as hunger or thirst. The way God has chosen to allow us to fulfill this desire is through the expression of sexual intercourse in marriage. When we allow our God-given desire for sexual expression to be hooked up with a lust-filled thought for anyone other than our mate, the tempter's voice loudly and clearly gives directions on how to proceed.

Satan is "a murderer . . . he is a liar, and the father of it" (John 8:44). He would like everyone to be a drunkard or an adulterer or anything else that is an abomination to God.

Learning to Guard Your Heart

Before we were "born again" (John 3:3), God's Word says we could not even *see* the Kingdom of God—never mind *enter into* it. We were living by our Adamic nature, and we were not controlled by the Spirit of God. But the Bible tells us when the Spirit of God takes over a life, we become "a new creation; the old has gone, the new has come!" (2 Corinthians 5:17,

NIV). Our inner man no longer must submit to the bondage of sinful, fleshly desires.

Our physical body, however, was not redeemed or made new. We must wait for this promise to be fulfilled at the resurrection. Our physical appetites are still there and must be mastered by the new creation we have become—children of God.

"Keep thy heart [appetites] with all diligence; for out of it are the issues of life" (Proverbs 4:23).

If your appetites were already made perfect, you would not have to guard them.

Ideas originating in our flesh rather than our spirit still come to us—ideas for evil and strong imaginings. When we begin to desire someone who isn't ours, we move from the normal quickening of a healthy, sexual appetite into the area of "lusting after."

"Ye have heard that it was said by them of old time, Thou shalt not commit adultery: But I say unto you, That whosoever looketh on a woman [or a man] to lust after her [him] hath committed adultery with her [him] already in his [her] heart" (Matthew 5:27–28).

Satan is always waiting for us to play into his hands. He knows when we have refused to guard our hearts and when we have allowed our desires to become off-limits in "lusting after" another. That's when he gets an opening to carry his plot further.

The Cookie Caper Syndrome

To help you better understand this business of "lusting after," let me tell you how my son Jeff at four years old preached the temptation message to his brothers and twin sister and anyone else who was around. "If your mommy has told you not to take a chocolate chip cookie from the cookie jar," he said, "then you better not do it because that's sin. If she comes into the kitchen and finds your hand in the jar, you are in BIG trouble!"

Now let's describe this story in adult terms. Let's imagine that one of your friends has just dropped by with a tray of cookies to be used for a mission luncheon. You glance at the cookies, thank her, and set them on your kitchen table. Every time you walk past that tray, the freshly baked aroma from those cookies makes your mouth water. What a variety, you say to yourself. Before long, you begin to zero in on one particular chocolate chip cookie. That one cookie has your attention. You think how good it would taste, and you begin to rationalize. "Oh well, one bite won't hurt."

The problem is you have just started a new diet. Plus, those cookies are not for you, as Potiphar's wife was not for Joseph. The cookies are for the missionaries coming for the luncheon. You have your own cookies in the pantry. Potiphar's wife was for Potiphar. Those cookies are an absolute no-no, but your desires have overridden your restrictions. Temptation has taken hold. You reach out, break off the brown edge, and place the tiniest bite in your mouth. One tiny bite—but oh-h how good it tasted. Now you go back and shove the whole cookie in your mouth.

Let's make this illustration even more adult. What if you were sitting in a room with ten different men, each one unique in appearance and each one wearing a marvelous after-shave lotion. But only one of them catches your eye. He's your chocolate chip cookie. He's lightly tanned, has large brown eyes, and smells so-o good. Remember that cookie with large, brown chips staring back at you and smelling so-o good?

Only now, in this instance, your problem is not in picking up that cookie and tasting it and wishing you hadn't because of your diet. Now your problem is that you desire a man who does not belong to you, which is far worse than simply desiring a forbidden chocolate chip cookie.

The rationalization with the cookie—"Oh well, just one bite won't hurt"—has now turned into temptation for this man.

Rationalization reinforces desire.

The crisis has arrived when you break off that brown edge of the cookie. How unimportant it seems—certainly not an action that would call for a sermon on gluttony. "This is so-o good," you say. "I'll eat the whole cookie, and no one will ever know. It's so good, I don't even feel guilty about eating it."

You have now *touched* and *tasted* for the first time, however, what you had only thought of before.

When you reach out, touch his arm, ruffle his hair, or pat his cheek, you taste the brown edge of the cookie. Your temptation increases in strength. With each little bite, your conscience becomes seared allowing you to carry this temptation one step further.

Opening the door to temptation is like opening a floodwall of sin.

First Timothy 6:17 says that God has "given us richly all things to enjoy." God has, indeed, given us all things to enjoy. This verse does not apply, however, when that enjoyable thing or person does not rightfully belong to us.

"There is a way that seemeth right unto man, but the end thereof are the ways of death" (Proverbs 16:25).

Sweet Suppression

Until I hit thirty-five, I could eat all the sweets I wanted without adding pounds to my thin frame. Now, I must guard not only my heart but my weight also! The problem is I LOVE sweets.

I had decided that the way to handle this problem was to eliminate buying all goodies. But my family banded together and told me in no uncertain terms, "No way!!" So I came up with another solution. I said, "Okay, you can bring those sweets into the house, but you must hide them from me. I don't want to see them, smell them, or touch them."

We had a large home with many closets, bureaus, cabinets, and brilliant hiding places. But do you know what? I always found those hidden treasures. I spent a lot of time and energy, which I could have used for more creative channels, sniffing out those hidden sweets.

Trying to kill my appetite by eliminating any trace of my temptation proved futile. My tendency to gain weight was no reason to destroy all sweets. I tried to kill my passion by pushing it underground and stomping on it.

Suppressing a temptation by hiding all the evidence is not the answer. Sweets are here to stay - and so are other men.

"Sexual responses and feelings should be accepted and not denied. Repressive denial can lead to volcanic explosion later on."[2]

Do you understand how my struggle with sweets relates to your appetite in the area of sex? Bait is being offered to us all the time. What should we do if we are aware that someone is becoming very appealing to us? Deny that we feel that way? Hide from ourselves? Suppress those desires so that no one could possibly guess what is going on in our mind? That would be the same as having had Bernie hide the candy from me. I knew it was there all the time. In fact, hiding it only made me think more about it. I had to learn how to deal with the problem rather than suppress my desire for it.

One *Virtue* magazine writer said,

The unmentionable temptation [sexual lust] grows best when pushed into the basements of our minds. It flourishes in the dark atmosphere of embarrassment about our sexuality and in our attempts to suppress it.[3]

We do not have to fear external temptations. Nor should we be like the little girl who diligently saved every nickel and dime to buy her mother a bottle of perfume. Every night she would kneel by her bed and pray, "Dear God, help me save enough money for that perfume, and please don't let the Girl Scouts come knocking at my door selling cookies."

God will protect us from the temptations that would like to come "knocking at our door" if we will make the right choices regarding our God-given appetites.

We are indeed "fearfully and wonderfully made" (Psalm 139:14). God made us with a built-in sexuality, and we cannot close our eyes to its reality.

Don't Build a Nest

Having said all the above, I hope I have fully convinced you that temptation itself is not sin. It only becomes sin when we entertain the idea or follow through with the deed. "Then when lust hath conceived, it bringeth forth sin" (James 1:15).

Thoughts of overindulging a normal appetite may come to a person one hundred times a day, but unless you welcome it into your heart, it remains just an irritating thought.

Don't feel guilty if a sexual thought comes into your mind. Don't come under condemnation if a member of the opposite sex touches you and you feel a rush of emotion. Recognizing the rugged good looks or tremendous personality of another man is not "lusting after." Lust is birthed when you magnify in your mind, dwell on special thoughts, or intend to have that *other* man as your own.

Finis Dake's comment in the Dake Bible defines lust as "continual longing, with the mind made up to commit the act if at all possible." In other words, let the bird fly over your head, but don't build a nest for him.

No guarantee comes with marriage that a woman will never have a sexual thought about another man. A woman once said to me, "I really thought that once I was married, I'd have eyes for no other person than my husband. But I find that I am not immune to thinking about other men."

Lewis Smedes of the Fuller Theological Seminary wrote,

> There is a difference between the awareness of someone's sexual attraction and being dominated by a desire to be intimate. Jesus did not draw a line between them, but we should know that there is a difference, so that we will be neither too quick to feel guilty, nor too careless with our feelings.

Both married and single women have become enraptured with male celebrities. Those men have charisma! They have charm! They have talent! But the truth is, while they are marvelous men to look at, they pose no real threat to our ever entering into sexual sin with them. The danger in this instance lies not in the bedroom but in the headroom.

When I met that Israeli man from Baltimore, I knew he was charming! To deny that would have been a lie. But the relationship never became a problem until I wanted to have a special place in that man's thoughts. When I began to dress in such a way that I knew would meet his approval, the temptation had already begun to progress.

Yes, some men are sexually stimulating. Recognizing those qualities is a normal observance. But once we have observed, the thought will leave our mind as we go to other things. We do not have to allow our imaginations to run away.

What to Do Before Temptation Comes

Let's lay some sound groundwork now on how to build a foundation for your faith that will not crumble with the weighty matters of life.

The primary building block is to understand that God has chosen us; we have not chosen Him. Individually, God sought us, found us, and redeemed us.

"Ye have not chosen me, but I have chosen you, and ordained you, that ye should go and bring forth fruit, and that your fruit should remain" (John 15:16).

God did not send Jesus to shed His blood upon a cross as a sacrifice for our sins only to introduce us to Him. God came to *stay* with us—to build an everlasting, eternal relationship with us. He promised never to leave or forsake us.

That means that God will never forsake us *especially* when we need Him most—in the midst of breaking down sin, which arises from within.

"God is faithful, who will not suffer you to be tempted above that ye are able; but will with the temptation also make a way to escape, that ye may be able to bear it" (1 Corinthians 10:13).

If we look into the temptations of Joseph, David, and Jesus, we see that David was the one who came to know what was in his heart *after* following his fleshly desires with Bathsheba. Joseph refused the temptation and ran from Potiphar's wife. Jesus said, "The prince of this world cometh, and hath nothing in me" (John 14:30). But David had to go back to God and say, "Against thee, thee only, have I sinned, and done this evil in thy sight. . . . Create in me a clean heart, O God; and renew a right spirit within me" (Psalm 51:4,10).

The apostle Peter (and Joseph and Jesus by example) told us the ways and means to deal with temptation *before* we encounter it. He speaks in 2 Peter 1:2–8 about building up our faith, growing in godliness, and becoming partakers in the divine nature of God. These provisions of faith building, Peter said, were meant for us so that we may escape "the corruption that is in the world through lust."

Here's the list which at first glance may bore you, but realize the Holy Spirit inspired Peter to make the list; therefore it is of utmost importance to consider it worthy of reflection.

1. We must first have **diligence**. We cannot rest on our salvation experience. In order to make progress in our spiritual maturity, we must be industrious and diligent in our desire to know God and live a life worthy of His calling. Joy Dawson, international Bible teacher, once said. "Some of as are diligent seekers of God, but others are only casual inquirers."

2. We must develop **faith** in our walk. Since faith comes by hearing God's Word, time must be allowed during our busy days to hear that Word. Sunday morning worship services are not the only way to do this. Both the Old and the New Testaments have been recorded on cassette tapes and can be played in your car or in your kitchen. In doing so, you will hide God's Word in your heart that you might not sin against Him.

3. Then **virtue** or clean living should be culti-vated. "A virtuous woman is a crown to her husband; but she that maketh ashamed is as rottenness in his bones" (Proverbs 12:4). A virtuous woman strives for the highest moral conduct. Obviously, this characteristic is not an inherited trait and must be cultivated in today's decadent moral climate.

4. **Knowledge** is another means to prevent us from falling into temptation. The psalmist prayed, "Teach me good judgment and knowledge" (Psalm 119:66). Knowledge is power—power we can use to defeat our enemy, Satan. We must gain knowledge of who God is and what His purposes are. We must also know Satan's tricks and how he uses them in temptation. In the next chapter, we'll also learn why it is necessary to know ourselves.

5. Peter tells us **self-control** must be added to our Christian walk. Early in life we learned that we could not have everything we wanted. Contrary to what the media and advertising promote, it is possible to live a satisfying and happy life without meeting our every whim. Learning to wait for something you really want or putting aside your selfish desires for the good of others is a step in learning self-control.

6. **Patience** or endurance is another quality that, if learned early, will prevent us from becoming engulfed in a trial. We cannot be like the woman who prayed for patience—right now. Humanity knows so little about God's perfect timing. If you are praying that God would perfect the character flaws in your husband, then give God time to work them out. God's timing works on the highest love for all concerned. Don't go looking for someone who is already "perfected" because there is no one.

7. **Godliness** is a much-discussed subject today but a little-practiced art. One of the best books on this subject is *The Practice of Godliness* by Jerry Bridges, who wrote, "Train yourself to be godly." Since unbelievers are godless people, surrounding yourself with mature, godly Christians will encourage you in your faith.

8. **Brotherly kindness**, a tender affection toward others, should also be added to our list of helps. Kindness causes us to be sensitive to the needs of others and to see God's blessings happen in their

lives. Lust is the opposite of brotherly kindness. Lust creates havoc, destroys relationships, and leaves long-lasting effects on people. But kindness leads people to repentance.

One discipline that will help you learn brotherly kindness is to look for opportunities to do good to others, both inside and outside the home. Busy hands are not idle hands. Doing good for others also occupies your mind, preventing you from dwelling on tempting thoughts.

9. Lastly, Peter exhorts us to develop **charity** or a love of goodwill toward all mankind. Again this involves self-sacrifice. Make it a practice to look for ways to love others. Certainly your family and church come first—but what about others in the community—those for whom Christ died but who know nothing of His love for them. Maybe you could volunteer to visit those in a nursing home and read Scripture to the bedridden. Maybe you could volunteer to baby-sit a neighbor's child while she attends a Bible study in your area.

Peter ends his list by saying in verse nine, "He that lacketh these things is blind, and cannot see afar off."

We do not want to be blind. We want to see afar off. We want to see when temptation is coming so that we may be alert, prepared, and ready to do battle. Blindness in battle means defeat.

We know "the wages of sin is death" (Romans 6:23), but do we know the *ways* of sin? Sin seems pleasing at first, but the longer we are in sin, the easier it is to stay in sin. It then becomes comfortable; happening more often until it becomes a habit that we have convinced ourselves is okay. We feel no shame and finally we convince ourselves that we need not repent.

5

Know Thyself

"By far the most momentous miscalculation I made was to assume that being in love with my husband meant I could not fall in love with anyone else. The second mistake, following hard on the first, was the belief that as long as I didn't have sex with anyone other than my husband, I wasn't really having an affair.—Eventually we began kissing. I felt like the worst caricature of a lovesick teenager. I only wanted to follow my desires, yet I was convinced this was terribly wrong. That conviction began to lose its intensity, though. Perhaps as the shock wore off, I became accustomed to my sins."
—*Anonymous*

One of the greatest mistakes we as women make is that we simply do not know ourselves. We do not understand our biological makeup; neither are we aware of the little female things we do consciously or subconsciously that cause us trouble. God made us females, and femaleness makes up our very fiber.

A friend recently said to me, "Judy, I *do* know a little about myself. I know I'm easily aroused sexually, and I know I arouse others easily. It's probably because I'm sensitive to people that I cause this response." This friend who thinks she knows a *little* knows a *lot* about herself. In knowing how she reacts, she is able to prevent a multitude of unpleasant situations.

"Good understanding giveth favour: but the way of transgressors is hard" (Proverbs 13:15, *italics added*).

My friend Walter Boice, an experienced counselor, voiced, "I think an open, warm person, a woman who is outgoing, gets along well with people, and is a good communicator, ought to be *aware* that she will draw the attention of men. She needs to be very careful how she interrelates with them. I don't think she should stop being open, warm, and loving or make herself look like a homely person. She just needs to be moderate in everything she does."

Let's look at some of the areas in which a woman should know herself.

Romantic Responders

God has created women to be responders. H. Page Williams said, "A woman must have something to which to respond, because God has made her a responder."[1] The author goes on to say that when a man withholds love from his wife, he is actually withholding love from himself. If a woman responds openly and warmly to another man's advance, she often does so because she has had nothing to respond to in her own marriage.

But some women are perpetual romantics. They respond to the slightest hint of attention as being a romantic suggestion.

Some of these responses may occur involuntarily. A woman may respond warmly when she hears a certain song, receives a word of praise, or accepts a loving touch. But it is the *voluntary* responses we want to deal with. We can respond to our biology in a godly manner, or we can respond in an ungodly manner. For example, what would you do if you found yourself responding to someone other than your husband? Probably your first thought would be, I can't believe I feel this way. A once casual, friendly relationship may become a kindled fire within you. You may have had no intention of having these feelings, but now they won't go away.

Let's discuss those feelings. First, you are not accountable for your feelings. You are biologically made to have feelings. You may be responding in a normal and natural way.

Archibald Hart, associate professor of psychology at Fuller Theological Seminary in Pasadena, California, wrote:

> Sexual responsiveness is fundamentally instinctual, even though it is heavily influenced by factors of learning. It is based in biology with hormones that can powerfully control behavior and emotions. So the basic attraction to others should not concern us. It is quite normal.[2]

What we are accountable for, however, is how to follow through with those feelings and how to make right decisions.

Second, you need not be enveloped in fear over what is biologically taking place in your body. If you have had some training in God's Word and by His Holy Spirit, you'll know what to do and how to control and redirect those feelings through the proper channel—your husband. (See also Chapter 10.)

Several years ago, I was the only female speaker at a convention in a neighboring state. The speakers spent much time together at that convention. We ate breakfast, lunch, and supper together. After the evening meetings, we'd all sit around talking before we retired for the evening.

One evening the men were sitting around discussing Bible doctrine and other subjects that required heavy contemplating. I was really tired and did not feel like entering into a theological discussion at that hour of the night. One of the men, also a conference speaker, came over and struck up a conversation while we munched on some cookies.

Maybe we were both a little giddy after a long day of personal ministry, but we hit it off really well and thoroughly enjoyed each other's company. Neither of us was concerned whether we were having male-female, male-male, or female-female conversation. We were just relaxing and enjoying some light conversation.

After that evening, our friendship began to grow. I'd tell him what Bernie was like and all about my children, and he told me about his family and his ministry. He was warm and engaging. But neither of us allowed the conversation to get to any level of intimacy.

I *was* guarding my heart.

But as the week wore on, I looked forward to ending the day in more conversation and compan- ionship with this interesting man. My feelings had progressed from seeing him merely as a friend to instead having an intense mental suggestion: Wouldn't it be wonderful to know this man more intimately?

Apparently, I had allowed my guard to drop, and my biology *responded* to my mental assent. That evening, in my room, the intensity of my battle progressed as these thoughts of him stayed with me. I walked the floor and prayed. In desperation, I crumbled onto my bed and pounded my fists into the mattress. I cried out to God, "God, there is no way I can wake up tomorrow morning and function in the ministry. This thing has me so distracted, so overwhelmed because of the shock of it, and so ashamed at my own feelings. If I must face anybody, I know they will see in my eyes my inner struggle. I'm afraid to face him, too, Lord. And I'm even more afraid of the sweet pleasure of all of this. God, you know I cannot change my feelings or stop my emotions. My emotions will not listen to me. Please, Please, God, gather all Your troops and send angels to help. By the time I wake up in the morning, may I be what I was before this encounter with temptation. May my feelings be once again what they were when I came to this convention. God, my only hope is in You. I know there is grace available to me."

While I was praying, the thought came to me that this man may be going through the same struggle. Then I began to pray for his soul with the same intensity that I had been praying for my own— asking God not to permit Satan to attack or defeat either of us. "The Lord knoweth how to deliver the godly out of temptations" (2 Peter 2:9).

And on and on I went, finally falling asleep with my clothes still on.

When I awoke in the morning, I felt refreshed and strengthened. I knew that God had poured out His grace and His mercy upon me. At what hour, I did not know. But I also knew some disciplinary actions were required on my part in order to once again guard my heart.

God wanted me to live out, in a self-controlled manner, His righteousness. And so before I left my room, I made some decisions. Thank God I did not have to make these decisions based on my irrational emotions of the previous night. I made my decisions based on faith and facts rather than feelings. I decided to eat breakfast, lunch, and dinner at another table. Decreasing conversations alone with him, I got busy spending time getting to know the other speakers. But I did so in a manner not obvious to him, not wanting to raise the possibility of an encounter where he may ask me if something was wrong or if I was angry about something.

If my thoughts once again returned to the sweet feelings of the previous night, I did not try to suppress them. Instead, for the remainder of the conference I set my mind on something of worth and meaning for me. For instance, many had shared with me the deep and hurtful things going on in their lives. So I prayed for them and their needs. I also occupied my mind with details concerning packing, travel schedules, last minute phone calls, and other busy work I needed to do before I left.

Now I want to be honest so that those of you reading this know I truly identify with what temptation means. Several times during the day those thoughts would come back to me. What I had experienced was a real spiritual battle! I do not in any way mean to spiritualize or diminish how real the battle was.

What I do want to emphasize is that I was not in the battle alone. When the enemies of Israel, God's chosen people, came in a great multitude to battle against them, God gave Jehosaphat, king of Judah, a promise. He said, "The battle *is* not yours, but God's" (2 Chronicles 20:15).

We, too, are God's chosen people:

> Ye have not chosen me, but I have chosen you, and ordained you, that ye should go and bring forth fruit, and that your fruit should remain: that whatsoever ye shall ask of the Father in my name, he may give it you (John 15:16).

God's help and grace are available to us, His chosen, when we call out to Jesus our great High Priest.

> For we do not have a high priest who cannot sympathize with our weaknesses, but one who has been tempted in all things as we are, yet without sin. Let us therefore draw near with confidence to the throne of grace, that we may receive mercy and may find grace to help in time of need (Hebrews 4:15–16, *NASB*).

God taught me some lifelong messages that night about spiritual warfare and my own vulnerability. That is why each of us must know our own areas of vulnerability. Your emotions can be triggered to respond in a way you least suspect. Perhaps someone who now holds no interest for you, someone with whom you have a purely platonic relationship, may at a later time trigger your emotions and cause you to respond.

However, I am not saying that platonic relationships always lead to intimacy. But platonic relating upon platonic relating upon platonic relating can lead to a *desire* for intimacy.

That gentleman at the conference and I built upon our relationship daily. Had those conversations been spread out over several months rather than every day, I don't believe my body or my emotions would have responded in the way that they did.

God-given sexual responses are not sinful—unless we choose to let them become so.

The Manipulator

Some of us need to know about ourselves in another way—our *controlling* or *manipulating* tendencies. Dr. Louis McBurney said,

> Some women cherish a deep, inner hatred for men and a compulsion to gain control over them. Frequently they were rejected or abused by their fathers. Often they learned in childhood and adolescence that sensuality is their most effective weapon. Consciously or subconsciously, they form a pattern of conquests while they appear to be helpless women who need a strong man to care for them.[3]

Lot's two daughters are good examples of manipulating women. These women grew up with a father who was not a very good example to his daughters. First, Lot chose to live in the town of Sodom—a town full of utter degradation. And he chose a Sodomite as his wife—one who was thoroughly entrenched in the ways of corruption. When his daughters were still young girls, some heavenly guests visited their home. In the evening, the corrupt men of Sodom surrounded Lot's house and demanded that the visitors be brought out to them "so that we can have sex with them" (Genesis 19:5, *NIV*). Lot then made this ludicrous offer: "No, my friends. Don't do this wicked thing. Look, I have two daughters who have never slept with a man. Let me bring them out to you, and you can do what you like with them" (Genesis 19:7–8, *NIV*).

Lot's carelessness regarding his daughters manifested itself in their rebellion later on in a mountain cave. (See Genesis 19:31–36.)

Even though Lot and his daughters had left Sodom, Sodom had not left his daughters mentally.

Out of a sexual union with Lot, the firstborn daughter conceived a son named Moab. He was the progenitor of a nation that became the enemies of God's people— the Moabites. Moab's mother, who was Lot's daughter, had a controlling, haughty spirit. Haughtiness and control are closely related.

Satan also has a controlling and manipulating character. He didn't rise up against God because he thought of himself as ugly, dumb, or inferior. He rebelled because he actually thought he was equal with God. He was haughty. He wanted control. His attitude was, "If I can't control it all, forget it. It's better to reign in hell than to serve in heaven." And whammo—he fell.

"Pride goeth before destruction, and a haughty spirit before a fall" (Proverbs 16:18).

For some women, the only way they can win is to get control over a man and bring him down. However, he and she both topple in the crash.

Betsy Kylstra, a sensitive counselor friend, shares these potent remarks:

> When we talk about sexual lust the goal is sex. We want to be in the arms of that man. We want to be seduced and satisfied by that man. The same thing can be going on, however, without a sexual goal. That is the seduction of that man not for the purpose of sex, but to gain a special place in his heart. You want to be important to that man in power. But the dynamics are similar.
>
> First there is courting, and then there is seduction. But the latter is carried on in a more subtle fashion—through manipulation. Rationalization says, "Oh, I just want to help that person."
>
> Maybe he is the pastor or the employer. So he is courted, flattered, hugged, and told how great he is. Actually that man is being prostituted just as if we had him in our arms. We have used him in order

that we might find a special place in his heart. Many women are like that, and they know *exactly* what they are doing.

Walter Boice said, "If a woman's openness and warmness are actually used to manipulate men, then she needs to change. It may take a while to change, but she can definitely change."

As you are reading this, ask the Lord to show you your motives. Are they pure toward those men you admire and not shaded with a desire to control or manipulate?

The Dreamer or Fantasizer

Another good indicator to help us know ourselves is to examine our daydreams or fantasies. Each of us was created with the ability to daydream. For most people, daydreaming can be a healthy, psychological release. Daydreams allow us to relax, increase our ability to concentrate, help us develop creativity, and assist us in deepening our spiritual walk with God. There is nothing wrong with daydreaming about family vacations, a future home, etc.

Some women, however, have become captive to their daydreams as a psychological haven from a world in which they can no longer cope.

When a woman is not being emotionally satisfied in her marriage, she often begins to fantasize what another lifestyle may be like. Even though she may have a satisfying physical relationship with her husband, she still may feel deprived in the area of intimacy. She may be married to the strong, silent type who does not communicate or listen to what she is trying to say. Or she may be married to a selfish or demanding man who is a taker rather than a giver.

Therefore, rather than actually have an affair, this woman begins to daydream what it would be like if only. . . . Perhaps this woman has no particular man in mind at all. She simply has fantasized about the "other one." This could be termed "mental adultery."

I received a letter from a woman who allowed herself to fantasize as a vehicle of retaliation. Her husband was not sensitive in understanding or in meeting her emotional needs. So she got back at him through her mental fantasies. She wrote:

> I imagine that I have lost forty-five pounds from stress in making a decision to abandon my family and from the acute melancholy that I know will follow my decision. Then I imagine I put on a pair of blue jeans and matching jacket and follow around a western singing group. I hang out in the bars and dance to the hillbilly music while smoking, drinking, and talking. I see myself going home with one of the men from the bar and going to bed with him.

She told me she soon abandons this fantasy for several reasons. She realizes that she is in her forties and cannot keep up with such hard-hitting days and nights. "And if I continued in those ways," she said, "I know I would be on the road to hell."

She then proceeds to fantasize in a more gentle route—one in which her needs have been saturated and her venom vented.

> In this fantasy, I find a middle-aged guy—very ordinary—this is a key requirement. A beachcomber is the perfect type. He must be fairly unattractive so I don't have the pressure of much competition. In this fantasy, I don't even have to lose forty-five pounds.

This guy is crazy about me. He asks me about my every thought and feeling. He's interested in everything I do throughout the day. He comments frequently on my beauty. He loves to touch me. My voice and thoughts are more important to him than anything else on earth. We go to motels often.

I just go on living my normal life in this fantasy. I get my needs met, and I am "Miss Cool" around my husband. I'm never hurt, in need, or vulnerable to my husband because this "other man" makes up for what he lacks.

Now for those of you who have never fantasized, you may be unable to relate to this woman's way of escape. Thousands of women, however, do deal with their unmet needs in this way.

One woman's husband was warm, handsome, and intelligent and did meet her emotional needs—but he wasn't spiritual. That need caused her to daydream in great detail about what it would be like to be married to a spiritual giant.

Another woman told me how she fantasized during a particularly difficult time in her marriage. "When things got rough," she said, "I would wonder whatever happened to Dean or Bill or Larry—all those fellows I grew up with whom I could talk to about anything." She fantasized what life would have been like if she had married one of these men rather than her husband.

Each of these women entered into mental adultery through vivid imaginations. Had they been low in imagination, they may not have experienced this. The problem with fantasizing is that the men these women dream up are always perfect in their sight.

If you are having fantasies about someone else and want this to stop, whatever you do—*never tell the other person what has been going on in your mind.* Some have told themselves they should confess it to the one involved and that would end it. Some are curious to see whether the other person's feelings are mutual. One vivid imagination is enough!

When unmet needs are combined with day-dreams and fantasies, women become extremely vulnerable for an affair.

The Flirt

Another area women need to examine in themselves is *flirting*. This is an area where we most tend to rationalize by saying, "Oh, I really didn't mean anything by it. I was just being friendly."

Those who make light of flirting should consider the clincher for *not* doing it. Maybe flirting means nothing to the woman doing it, but *it may provoke that man to lust.* Your frivolity may indicate to that man that you are interested in more than a casual acquaintance. Certainly, this is one area that a married man or woman should never enter into. All too often it becomes the open invitation to a deeper relationship.

I asked Walter Boice, "What are the ways you have seen women flirt?"

"Well," he said, "the biggest way women flirt is through flattery. They say things such as 'How good you are,' 'How nice to be with you,' or 'You sure have all the answers.' This leaves the man vulnerable to further flattery.

"Another way women flirt is by the way they use their body language. She may touch or lean against him over a desk. She may show her legs when she sits opposite a man."

"How should a man react to a flirting woman?" I asked.

He said, "I recommend that men make a covenant with their eyes. It's biblical, you know. Job said, 'I made a covenant with mine eyes; why then should I think upon a maid?' " (Job 31:1).

I asked him how he applied this to his own life.

"For instance," he said, "if a woman moves or crosses her legs, I don't look. I've made a covenant with my eyes. It is a natural tendency for the eye to pick up movement. But a man must position himself so he does not use his eyes in the wrong way."

"A woman can also use her eyes incorrectly," he said. "I've seen women look a man up and down and then stare at him. If he looks back, she will use her eyes to speak volumes. This woman could be oppressed by a seducing spirit."

Using sexual humor may also cause vulnerability in a man.

Mel White wrote, "I know how subtly evil enters into the purest relationship, and how quickly sexual teasing and humor can lead to seduction and sexual lust."[4]

This kind of casual joking gets around easily and frequently even in Christian circles. Many became used to using sexual humor before they were Christians, and the habit remained.

A friend told me of an incident that caused her to battle with sexual thoughts for many days after it happened. A male friend phoned her home and asked for her husband.

"He isn't here right now," she answered.

"Oh, good," he said to her. "I'll be right over." Uncomfortable and unclean thoughts began to cross my friend's mind. What if he does show up? Has he been thinking about me? Why would he say that if there weren't a thread of suggestive truth in it? This woman had to get alone and pray away these strange feelings she was experiencing.

Sexual humor and teasing cannot be excused. Careless words can cause an enormous amount of problems for another person.

"Like a madman shooting firebrands or deadly arrows is a man who deceives his neighbor and says, 'I was only joking'" (Proverbs 26:18–19, *NIV*).

Examine yourself in these areas. Are your compliments sincere, or are they tinged with lustful feelings? Your words and movements may be quite innocent, but Satan could be setting you up as bait for a male who is starved for praise. He may have to make some tough decisions about going home to a critical wife or staying around a woman who gratifies his sagging ego.

The Holy Spirit is ever ready to help us understand ourselves. If we ask for His help, He will convict us if we are flirting either consciously or subconsciously. We need to use our godly friendliness wisely.

The Perfectionist

The woman with perfectionist qualities should also become acutely aware of these tendencies before problems develop. In this woman, perfectionism compels her to want more than she has. She, in fact, must have the perfect husband. She develops what I call the *Robert Redford Syndrome*. (Or the younger girls may substitute Brad Pitt, the older women may substitute Clark Gable, or the 106-year-old gal may substitute Rudolph Valentino . . . Who???) Let me explain what I mean. Robert Redford's reputation as a Hollywood Prince Charming is well known. He has good looks, money, intelligence, and personality. Most worldly women would agree these are the ideal features of manhood. Men with these "power tools" are popular, get good jobs, and attract women.

But Christian women should have different values in their choice of a companion. A Christian woman should be interested in a man who loves God with all his heart, soul, and mind. If he does not, how can this man lead his family in the ways of God and be a man of prayer and of the Word?

My husband was very appealing to me, and an understanding man of God. He was also a great listener. Whenever I needed him, he made time for me. At one time, Bernie practiced law and had one of the largest clientele in Baltimore. Why? Because he was so brilliant? No, it was because he listened to his clients. He would counsel and advise them over the phone, sometimes for hours, and listen, really listen, to their problems.

Bernie would laugh with me, get teary-eyed when I told him how God moved in someone's life, and gave me oodles of time to explain myself. He was my closest friend, my buddy, and my brother in the Lord.

But Bernie was not Robert Redford. What man really is? When I am teaching this subject in a seminar, I have asked the question, "Who thinks she is married to a Robert Redford?" No one has ever raised her hand, except once.

In surprise, I asked this woman, "How long have you been married?"

"Three weeks," she replied. The audience chuckled.

It took longer than three weeks for me to discover that Bernie was not Robert Redford. This marvelous man of God could not change a light bulb with finesse. Several times, he left the metal part in the socket and removed only the glass. Once we had to have an electrician come and remove the entire chandelier as a result of Bernie's attempt to change the bulb.

Another time, we had just purchased a new, red, self-propelled, electric lawn mower from Sears. Up until this time, Bernie had delegated grass cutting to our three sons or a handyman. But since no one was available and the grass demanded attention, Bernie decided to tackle it himself. I stood behind a glass patio door watching him, so proud of the way he was beautifully pruning our lawn.

But then something went wrong. Apparently a stubborn weed refused to be plowed over by the lawn mower. Bernie let go of the handle, bent down to pull out the weed by hand, and the lawn mower continued on its way. I watched in frustration, yelling at Bernie who could not hear me over the sound of the motor, as the mower plunged over the seawall and into the lake.

Bernie didn't have it all together in the fix-it area either. Once we had a toilet that would flush all by itself when no one was in the bathroom.

It was a joke to the children, and me, but it was a real mystery to Bernie. The plumber charged us $37.78 for the twenty seconds it took to install a small rubber plunger.

Another thing bothered me about Bernie. He hated broccoli. Unfortunately, he had relayed the message to our children, and they wouldn't eat any either. My friends had children who all ate their greens. But did mine? No—all because Bernie hated broccoli. When I made a casserole, we played a game at our house called "Who can find the hidden broccoli first?"

I could tell you a lot more about Bernie, but he wouldn't want me to go any further than the broccoli. Rest assured, I was not married to someone the world would call a Prince Charming. Neither are you. But many a gal is married in her heart to another simply because he has a power tool that her husband lacks.

When a perfectionist tries to find a solution for her needs and leaves her mate for her "Robert Redford," it will only be a matter of time before she will find him disappointing also. No man can meet every need in a woman. If he could, a woman would have no need to depend on God for her joy and fulfillment.

Maybe that's why God leaves each of our partners with some inadequacies. >grin<

Resurrected Lives

If you know that you are a responder—if you know your own areas of secretive manipulations and that romantic daydreams are all part of your femaleness—you can prevent sinful situations from occurring.

All of us were created sexual beings, and sexual stimuli surround us daily. But not every woman, thank God, becomes a victim to an affair.

Why? She has learned the secret of knowing herself and preparing herself by putting on the full armor of God, which I will cover in the following chapters.

If we truly desire to have resurrected lives, we cannot rationalize sin in any area. My close friend and confidante, Jo Anderson, put it this way: "Because we know our needs, we cannot bend the Word of God to meet those needs. We cannot rationalize sin by saying, 'God wants my needs met; I want my needs met; so I'll bend God's Word, and He won't mind.' What God wants is for death to work in us—He wants us to apply the cross. What is the cross? It's the point where my will crosses His will."

God wants to resurrect new life in us.

While only God knows what is in each woman's heart, we, when we are made aware of our own special problem areas, can and must allow God to replace those potentially sinful ways with wholesome and holy character traits.

6

Causes of Infidelity

"Sometimes I think the first element in sin is irrationality. *I have this warm feeling. It must be from God. Therefore it's okay.* And from then on, we're not thinking straight at all."—David Seamands[1]

Someone once said that having an affair is like taking an amphetamine. It promotes a short-time high but does not cure any problems. Why then do some women wind up swallowing that bitter pill of unfaithfulness? In this chapter, we'll look at some of the reasons women have taken a detour that has led them out of God's will.

I don't believe any Christian woman sets out with the intention to commit sin. In fact, many women will not consciously be able to explain their actions. "I don't know why it happened, it just happened," is a common remark. But no one wakes up one morning and by that afternoon has *fallen* into an affair. When women enter into an affair, it is usually to satisfy a long-standing, unmet, emotional need rather than a sexual need.

Cecil Osborne said, "Each of us has a threefold drive: to be loved unconditionally, to change others so that life will be easier for us, and to have all of our needs met."[2]

Two conditions usually exist in a woman's life before events progress to the place of sin. One of them is that, even though a woman is a professing Christian, she is living a carnal lifestyle. The other condition is that a woman has a seared conscience. From these two traits, spring great evil.

Let me define these conditions. A *carnal believer* is a "babe(s) in Christ" (1 Corinthians 3:1) or one who is immature in her walk with the Lord. She is more likely to become involved in infidelity than those who have a vital, alive, daily walk with God. Carnal women have a tendency to be more influenced by their "glands" than the committed Christian who is ruled by God's Word hidden in her heart. (See Psalm 119:11.)

Several clues help identify carnality. The Bible says, "You are still worldly" and "acting like mere men [women]" (1 Corinthians 3:3, *NIV*). When a Christian woman looks, acts, and sounds like a worldly woman, you can be sure she is still living with one foot in the Kingdom and one foot in the world. She may spend endless hours in shopping malls, antique shops, or dress shops, feeding her materialistic drive for possessions. Her reading material may be unprofitable to her maturity, and her leisure afternoon hours may be spent in front of television soap operas.

A woman only reaps what she sows. If she plants corn, she'll reap corn. If she plants carnality, she'll reap carnality.

Checkpoints for a Clear Conscience

A woman with a *seared conscience* is one who feels no guilt or sorrow when she has done wrong. Many women who have shared how they become involved in an affair said something like this: "When I married my husband, I was not saved. So, therefore, I am not committing adultery by loving this new man who is a believer. My relationship to God has never been better than it is now, and we are not wrong in loving each other." No sorrow, hurt, or personal remorse is expressed. Guilt and conscience have been seared in this woman.

Ken Sumrall, president of Church Foundational Network, helped me to see the importance of a good conscience. He said, "It takes the power of the Holy Spirit to keep people from doing wrong. If the conscience has died or has been 'seared with a hot iron,' (1 Timothy 4:2) then it's impossible to hear God any more. God's moral laws never change. They are the absolutes in the universe. God will judge this nation unless there is a restoration of conscience."

To prevent infidelity from unleashing itself upon us, we must have a conscience that bristles with life and is sensitive to God's direction. If we do not keep our consciences void of offense between God and us, they will become weak and seared; and the windows of heaven, from which blessings flow, will be shut.

How can we determine if our conscience is alive and well? Ken Sumrall suggests the following points. We must *know* that all sin grieves God's heart. "If I regard iniquity in my heart, the Lord will not hear *me*" (Psalm 66:18). We must know that wrong is wrong, even if we do not get caught. Fantasizing and/or secret phone calls or meetings fall into this category. Finally, we must know that wrong is wrong even if the government has legalized it. "Thou shalt not follow a multitude to do evil" (Exodus 23:2).

For the sake of prevention, pray that God will make you sensitive to what displeases Him. Ask Him to give you a lively conscience that warns you when you begin to rationalize and excuse yourself over wrongdoing.

Let's look at some areas where carnality and seared consciences cause problems to originate.

Romantic Longings

I laughed at this story that supposedly took place in the Garden of Eden. After many days of suppressing her curiosity, Eve asked Adam, "Adam, do you love me?"

"What'd you say, Eve?"

Eve repeated, "I asked if you love me."

"Who else?" Adam replied.

Women have asked that serious question ever since. My friend, Carl, says, "A husband needs to spend time talking with his wife; otherwise, she'll find someone else to talk with. *Have you ever wondered why Eve got into a conversation with a serpent?*" Interesting!

In the beginning of a marriage, both partners are usually charged with high emotional intensity. Asking the other if he/she loves you isn't necessary. There is usually enough romantic expression to satisfy both partners.

After a few years, however, the male is usually content with having his basic needs met—food, sex, a clean home, and well-behaved children. (Not necessarily in that order.) But the female continues to desire the highly romantic aspect of their relationship. Dr. James Dobson attributes this romantic need to "genetic influences implemented by the hypothalamus region in the brain" and probably from early experiences as a little girl.

The problem begins when the husband either remains uninformed of this romantic longing in his wife or chooses to refuse to meet that need. When a woman in this situation has a lukewarm relationship with God, her first instinct is not to turn to Him in prayer, trusting the Lord to see her through. Her carnal instincts may direct her to find fulfillment vicariously through soap operas and/or secular romance books.

Sharon Kaye shared one morning on the *700 Club* how soap operas almost broke up her marriage. "The women on the soaps became my models," she said. She began to act like those women on the screen. Eventually, self-will and domination became her outstanding traits.

One man told a friend that he could walk into a grocery store at 4 pm any afternoon and have any woman he wanted. "If she has been watching soaps all day and then runs out to pick up something for dinner, she's all stirred up and ready for some romance in her life," he said.

Maybe this man has made a huge exaggeration about women, but I wonder if there is more truth in that than we dare accept!

Malcolm Muggeridge once commented that television in particular but media in general is the greatest single influence in society today. What are Christian women reading these days? Well, I haven't seen many women carrying around the great Christian classics on prayer and faith written by Moody, Finney, or Spurgeon. But I've seen a lot of light, romantic novels tucked away in handbags.

In 1991 Harlequin books sold more than 200 million romance novels worldwide. A survey conducted by a Christian publishing company showed fifty-two percent of the women polled bought romance novels regularly.

"I found that reading romance novels presented a serious stumbling block to me," one woman said. "I have a tendency to be overly sentimental, and those love stories were making me *restless* and dissatisfied with my life."

This kind of fiction is designed to arouse our emotions. The problem is, however, that fiction makes romance, love, and marriage look more exciting than they really are. Vicarious sexual arousal makes one's present situation seem pale by comparison. No real-life marriage can stand up to fictional romanticism—even if it is labeled Christian romance.

And how about those women's magazines with the attractive cover girl on the front?

"Years ago," one woman told me, "I was in a dress shop waiting for a salesperson. A popular woman's magazine sat on a table beside me. I picked up the magazine and opened it to the article "Better Sex For Women." I sat down and read the entire article. I read all those new ideas, techniques, surveys, and explicit details, and I was hooked. I thought I had a good marriage until I read that article, and then great dissatisfaction hit me. It lasted for a long time and did not lift from me until I did some very serious crying out to God alone."

For various reasons, many married women who have not experienced romance for an extended period—either sexual or emotional—may be stimulated by this vicarious lifestyle, causing them to want a "real" man in their arms. When a woman reads a stimulating article such as the above example, she may create within herself an idealistic situation—too idealistic even for the happily married.

By purposely availing ourselves of the "sensuous stuff" being offered today we may well cause ourselves increased sentimentalism or dissatisfaction with our situations rather than supplying us with light relaxation or entertainment.

Recapturing Youth

Restlessness sometimes arises out of a need for reaffirmation. A woman who has always been admired for her outer beauty may long to hear those compliments in order to find fulfillment in life. Her need to live in her good looks has caused her to become vulnerable.

An intense restlessness sometimes occurs in women after the age of forty. This intensity comes not especially from wanting to hear what a magnificent specimen of womanhood she is, but simply because she desires to hold onto her femaleness in general. This cry for reaffirmation is a result of physical changes in her body—bulging tummy, sagging skin on her upper arms, wrinkles, and graying hair.

My mother helped me solve this aging problem quite well. She said, "Judy, when people ask you how old you are, tell them you are fifteen years older than you are. They'll walk away commenting on how young you look rather than how old you look." You have to know my mother to understand her wonderful sense of humor. Actually, I love growing older. With each birthday, I grow one year closer to going "Home."

During this middle stage of life, a woman may become increasingly flirtatious. What she is actually saying is, "I won't let time cheat me out of my sexuality." Subconsciously, women want to be capable of stirring up the opposite sex again. When these mid-life feelings are combined with mid-life monotony in marriage, the possibilities for infidelity increase.

One white-haired woman came up to me after I had taught on this subject and said, "When a woman is menopausal, she can expect to experience some rather strange emotions. Those unusual emotions should not surprise us though because the female hormones are decreasing and the male hormones are increasing."

As bizarre as this may seem to you, some women may even find themselves involved in mental adultery with their daughter's boyfriend. A recent letter to Ann Landers revealed one woman's predicament. She said, "I am a professional woman in my mid-40's and have been married for over 20 years." She went on to tell how a handsome young man over six feet tall, tan, with blue eyes and blond hair had been visiting her teenage daughter.

One day he stopped by the house when the daughter was away. After about an hour of light conversation with the mother, the young man got up to leave. Then he said, "I'm going to do something I've been wanting to do for a long time." And he kissed her fully on the lips. She made no effort to stop him. "In fact," she said, "I enjoyed it a great deal . . . and now I am mentally obsessed with this kid. I can't believe this is happening to me!"

Ann Landers advised this woman that her problem was not unique. Many others in the same situation had written to her. Ann's advice to this woman was to find a competent counselor to help her think rationally.

But for some women, counseling may present still another set of problems.

Rationalized Transferences

Archibald Hart wrote:

> If you were hungry for love, wouldn't it be nice to find someone who was well-educated, mannerly, articulate, but also a good listener, respected in the community, occupationally powerful, yet unselfish, and willing to spend time alone with you for free?[3]

Where else could you find such a person but in your own church office? And in finding him, many women rationalize that they don't want the counselor's *solution* to their problems—THEY WANT THE COUNSELOR HIMSELF. Pastors and church counselors have faced this distressing problem many times in their ministry. The technical term when a client projects feelings and desires into the counseling relationship is called *transference.*

Counseling situations may then be another cause for a strong, emotional, sexual relationship to develop.

I received this letter describing what one woman experienced:

> I had to go to my pastor for much counseling, and often we would be alone for long periods of time. He was the first person who ever really showed genuine concern for me.
>
> After a while, I started getting a crush on him. I never called it lust because at first I didn't think sexual thoughts. But before long, I started having "weird" thoughts that concerned something happening to his wife, and he and I getting together. After my emotions ran their course, I repented. Thank God it was no more than that.

Counter-transference happens when *both* the client and the counselor project their needs into the counseling session. When both of them are emotionally and romantically starved, lust (or what they believe is love) can destroy what started out to be an innocent professional relationship. And if a minister or counselor can be swayed because of his own crisis level, the possibility exists for the relationship to become sexual even though it may remain in the emotional realm for a great length of time.

Intimacy, not necessarily sexual intimacy, is a by-product of continued counseling between opposite sexes. Dr. James Smith, director of family life development at Highland Park Presbyterian Church in Dallas, Texas, said:

> God designed us so that sexual tension would increase with intimacy. A lot of Christian leaders are not cautious in this area. We probably all know someone who has suffered devastating heartbreak and had to leave the ministry because of entering into a counseling situation without proper safeguard.[4]

Pastor friends of mine have another woman in the office who is praying during the counseling appointment. Or some pastors leave their office door open.

The best "affair prevention" method in this case is quite simple. For both parties, it is always best to maintain a professional attitude. Pray that God will help you with your emotions as you share your areas of vulnerability with the counselor. If all else fails and you find your emotions becoming too strong, don't hesitate to find another counselor.

Rejection

Another major problem area that may lead to improper sexual response is past rejection.

Walter Boice, again through his extensive counseling experience, shed some light on this cause. He said:

> Much of the root problem of lust stems from rejection from parents, primarily the father. It may also be a combination of rejection from brothers or

boys at school. But when the father has rejected a daughter, she rebels. Many times her rebellion leads to promiscuous living and perhaps drug and alcohol abuse.

Until that woman can be set free through forgiving, she may continue to search for someone who will love her with an unconditional love. If a woman with great rejection problems marries and has not found love in the Lord and realized her position in Christ, the possibility exists that she'll continue on in her lifestyle still looking for that love she has not received in childhood.

Rejection causes feelings of insignificance, and this may add a hundred thousand more complexities to the relationship of two people.

Dr. Paul Meier says, "As a Christian psychiatrist, I have gradually become convinced that a lack of self-worth is the primary factor that limits our ability to love our mates intimately."[5]

Limited intimacy with our partner leaves us in emotional deprivation. Sometimes a woman believes she can find this intimacy with another person. That is deception, however, because it is her own feelings of insignificance that prevent her from having an intimate relationship with anyone.

Perhaps a woman has not been rejected in the past, but her husband has rejected her in a number of ways—some of them unintentionally. This causes feelings of unworthiness also. It may be that rejection has come from the absence of romantic love or emotional abandonment—where the husband has allowed work or other activities to come before his wife's needs.

One pastor's wife told me a story, which is the typical pattern leading women to look elsewhere for attention. She said, "My husband got so preoccupied with his work that he neglected me. Before long I began to feel unnecessary and unattractive. I felt estranged from him. Then I began to work with the husband of the couple in ministry with us. Needless to say, the attention that this male paid to me caused me to become vulnerable for an affair."

How true is the old saying, "No one can stand the awful knowledge that he/she is no longer needed."

Bernie and I reached a point in our marriage where he had become acutely aware of me. He'd say things like, "Judy, you sure look good in red" or "Mmm, you smell good." I asked him, "How come you've been so complimentary?" His answer was surely filled with wisdom. "Because," he answered, "I don't want you to have to look for compliments somewhere else."

Good advice for all husbands!

Fiery Darts

All the above causes may be traced to some root beginning—either a carnal lifestyle, a seared conscience, or from the results that spring from the circumstances we have discussed. I hesitate to include this subject in this chapter because of our humanness to look for motive "scapegoats." Yet I feel it is the one *most used* as the reason a woman enters into immorality.

God's Word tells us that *sometimes* we can receive a sneak attack, where by no predisposition of our own heart, we are hit by the "fiery darts of the evil one" (Ephesians 6:16). Now I'm not talking about causes that spring from a woman's own lifestyle but rather an unexplainable, unplanned impression upon one's mind.

Let's identify some of these fiery darts.

Perhaps one morning you awaken and realize that you have had an unclean dream involving yourself and someone other than your husband. Probably your first reaction is one of disdain and disgust. On the other hand, you may continue to hold onto the thought because of a desire to "figure this thing out."

Or, what if you are walking down the street, and, as Nat King Cole's old song went, "Crash, bam, alakazam, wonderful you walked by." All of a sudden you got a "shot in your biology," seemingly from left field, as a good-looking male walked by.

We can't use "the fiery dart" concept as a copout unless we have first examined our heart to see if we have given Satan a runway on which to land with these thoughts. But if we have examined our hearts and feel no conviction by the Holy Spirit, then there are some distinguishable marks to let us know the unclean thought has come from the enemy rather than from our own mind.

First, the suggestion comes suddenly—dart-like. Thoughts originating from our own hearts have a tendency to spring up more leisurely—sin is conceived line upon line.

Secondly, if a thought comes from our own heart, we tend to rationalize it as not being really so evil. But notions from Satan's heart to our mind startle and frighten our soul. We realize them as something terrible.

Lastly, when evil thoughts come from Satan, a mature Christian will loathe them and have a desire to resist them.

One couple recognized these fiery darts. Her husband relayed their experience to me:

Several months ago my wife began to tell me about harassing thoughts and dreams she was experiencing. She would not, however, tell me even the slightest detail. Her only comments were, "I don't know what to do—I really can't stand this. I wonder if other women have experienced this."

I was totally confused and helpless. One night I awakened and found her sitting in a chair in the living room crying and pounding her head with her fists saying, "Go away and leave me alone!"

I tried to pray with her and console her; and, for several weeks, she seemed fine. Before long, however, she began to have recurring bouts of harassment. She had even gone to the Christian bookstores seeking a book to help her find the freedom she desperately sought. But after attending the seminar you taught, she came home free, and full of joy. She still did not give me the details, but she experienced complete deliverance and freedom at those seminars.

I believe those flaming missiles from Satan were harassing this woman. In this case, I teach the line of defense from Ephesians 6:11–12:

Put on the whole armor of God, that ye may be able to stand against the wiles of the devil. For we wrestle not against flesh and blood, but against principalities, against powers, against the rulers of the darkness of this world, against spiritual wickedness in high places.

God's Word has given us the best defense against sin, whether it originates from our own heart or from an attack of Satan. Our directions are to gird ourselves with the truth of God's Word, to put on righteousness, to shod our feet with the gospel of peace, and to take the shield of faith.

When we have followed God's directions, He tells us we will be able to quench Satan's attacks, and we will be able to stand our ground in the evil day.

In this chapter, we have looked only at the *causes* of infidelity. I'll discuss practical, preventative measures in the chapters to follow.

7

Warnings from the Lighthouse

> "Immorality is the cumulative product of small
> mental indulgences and minuscule compromises,
> the immediate consequences of which were, at the
> time, indiscernible."—Randy Alcorn[1]

Up to this point we've discussed the world, the
flesh, and the devil's attack on what is God's most
holy covenant—the marriage relationship. I want to
deal in this chapter and in the remainder of the book
with the ways to incorporate an "affair prevention"
system into your life.

Most of us live what Dr. James Dobson calls
"The Straight Life"—cleaning sinks, mediating fights
between children, and driving the station wagon to
school and back twenty-three times a week. Without
some change of scenery, social interests, or hobbies,
life can at times be monotonous. But drifting from the
straight life in order to find something or someone to

fill the void leads to shipwreck when God is left out of the picture.

Jesus said, "I am the light of the world: he that followeth me shall not walk in darkness, but shall have the light of life" (John 8:12).

God never breaks His promises! If He promises to be our light, to lead us not into temptation and to deliver us from sin, that is exactly what He will do. But all God's promises come with a conditional clause: *if you will.* From His lighthouse, God will send us succinct danger signals sufficient to keep us from crashing on the jagged rock of sin—if we will only watch for them.

Let's look at some of the lighthouse signals.

The Warning Bells

In our station wagon was a gadget that went "ding, ding" whenever it wanted me to know something. It was a safety device that warned me something was wrong. Maybe I was supposed to check the seat belts, lock the doors, or check the rear gate. A quick glance at the electronic panel told me what was wrong so that I could correct it.

But after a while of listening to that ding, ding, it became easy to ignore. Sometimes I was completely oblivious to its warnings. If I wasn't observant, I could be headed for a dangerous situation. It would be great if after owning one of these new cars for a while, the ding-ding sound would change to a blaring siren. It would have the added dimension of causing us not to ignore something that had become commonplace to us.

The voice of the Holy Spirit is similar to that gentle reminder from my computerized car. "Uh-uh," He whispers to us. "Uh-uh, uh-uh," He repeats. And if we ignore the uh-uh long enough, His voice thunders,

"NO, NO." How merciful and longsuffering our Lord is to do this for us.

An interesting fact I noted was that all the women I had spoken to, without exception, who had become involved in an affair said that they *did* hear the voice of God warn them at the beginning. *But they chose to ignore it!*

When Jesus left the earth, He did not leave us alone to face innumerable opportunities for sin. He said, "Unless I go away, the Counselor will not come to you; but if I go, I will send him to you. When he comes, he will convict the world . . . of sin" (John 16:7–8, *NIV*).

First and foremost, a check from the Spirit of God is the strongest warning signal beamed out from Jesus, our Rock. We have settled for the moment, and one day we shall see the stupidity of settling for moments that may haunt and hurt our fragile hearts for years. Only the Spirit of God can open our eyes to the ruinous magnitude of what we are after or what we are doing.

The Drifting Alarm

A ship cannot simply drift into harbor. The captain must be knowledgeable and alert in order to guide his cargo safely into shore.

In Italy, there is a harbor that can only be reached by sailing through a narrow channel lined with dangerous rocks and shoals. Many ships have been wrecked there because of careless navigation. Consequently, three lights have been placed along the harbor to guide ships to safety. These three lights must line up and be seen as one light by the pilot before he can proceed safely into the harbor.

Disappointment, disillusionment, and despair are three warning alarms to watch for in your marital relationship. When the first alarm of disappointment sounds, it must be dealt with before it builds like layers of wax on a kitchen floor. One or two layers of wax are not as difficult to remove as eight or ten layers. Unfortunately, we do not take disappointments seriously nor see them as precursors to adultery.

If we fail to heed the first alarm, disillusionment and despair follow with their warnings that unless a change of course is taken immediately, disaster looms ahead.

In his book *Birthright,* David Needham says, "We become gripped with an obsession to sin when some other more respectable or righteous fulfillment in life is being frustrated." He calls this situation "a vacuum of meaninglessness." Needham explains that it is unthinkable to be alive without some degree of satisfaction in our lives and that we automatically reach out for a readily obtainable experience.

> That is why physical or sensory type lusts are so especially quick to arise. My vacuum of meaninglessness can be filled so immediately! There are times when stuffing my mouth satisfies. And for those moments life is making sense. Shallow sense, but then . . . any sense is better than an aching vacuum. . . . If the lust is sex, it may take a little while to find that person, that book or magazine, that "something" which will awaken that fantasy of meaning. I must consider my reputation of course, and my financial resources . . . it may require some careful planning and delay, but that's okay. For you see, from the very moment I set my mind on lust, *I am moving!* My mind is alive—planning, anticipating.[2]

If your marriage is drifting along like water-logged timber in a meaningless vacuum, it's time to take hold of the wheel and steer in a positive, God-directed channel. If we will first go to God and ask for wisdom and help, He promises to "fulfill the desire of them that fear him: he also will hear their cry, and will save them" (Psalm 145:19).

Too Much Togetherness

If you have ever seen ships waiting to go through a lock and dam, you know that only certain ones are chosen by the lockmaster. Obviously, not all the ships floating in the waiting area can come through at once.

So, too, God has given us someone with whom to travel through life. Can you imagine the havoc that would occur if each ship's captain decided to do his "own thing"? Disastrous situations arise when a man or a woman determines to travel through the rough waters with someone other than their chosen one.

In other words, a woman may find herself wanting to "channel" through life with someone other than her husband for any number of the reasons mentioned previously. Perhaps she has become attracted to a man either at work or at church, or it may even be the male partner of a couple with whom both she and her husband are friends. In any event, when she becomes aware of her attraction, time alone with that man should be avoided.

Let's look first at a togetherness problem among married women today that involves *working outside the home.* Friendships between a man and a woman are easily formed on the job because of common vision and interest. Combine these with the fact that working people often dress better, smell better, and communicate better than the mate who was left at home, and the working partner becomes even more appealing.

Over seventy percent of women are in the workplace. According to a popular women's magazine, sixty-eight percent of readers were involved in significant relationships that had been with someone at work.

A woman in daily contact with the opposite sex must be continually guarding her sexual appetites— especially if one or both are having problems with their mates.

When a male and a female look forward to sharing coffee breaks, lunches, and overtime together, it is time to look around for the warning signals. For those women who are really comfortable around men, enjoy being with them, and are forced into a continual relationship with them at work, the motto "Business As Usual" should be an unspoken law. Home should be where the heart is, and business should remain business.

In an issue of *Christianity Today*, Rodney Clapp said, "Some women are more comfortable with cross-sexual relationships than others. It is imperative that cross-sexual friendships be carefully maintained as friendships (not romances) and that passions remain in repose." I agree.

Too much togetherness may also occur in a *social setting*. It may be a very innocent occasion such as a church supper. That's how it started for Larry and Fran as they, with their spouses, sat next to each other at a pot luck supper.

"Where is your adorable little girl?" Fran innocently asked Larry.

"Oh, that's a sad story," Larry replied. "I don't want to ruin your dinner with my problems."

"No, tell me," Fran insisted.

And so he did. For almost an hour Larry shared with Fran how his first marriage ended in tragedy and now his darling daughter was in the middle of a custody battle. As Larry's eyes filled with tears, Fran felt certain it was God who had planned the seating arrangement so that she could console him.

"Oh, Larry," Fran said, "I, too, was married before, and my husband got custody of our two small children. I know exactly how you feel. I don't believe anyone can understand the hurt and loneliness one feels in this situation unless they have experienced it. I'll pray for you, and you pray for me."

Nothing wrong with that conversation, right!

Except that Fran began to feel a closeness to Larry that she had not experienced before. On continuous occasions, Fran and Larry found themselves discussing their mutual problems. One Saturday evening, at a social gathering with other couples, Fran sought out Larry and told him how often she had been thinking about him and praying for him. It was difficult to hear each other in a room full of people, so they stepped out onto the patio, under the moon and stars, and continued talking.

The next time they were together was at a committee meeting; only this time their mates were at home. When the meeting ended, they held hands and prayed along with the other committee members. What happened? Warmth, emotional feelings, and intimacy developed. The rest is history.

Author Jamie Buckingham said something once that I have never forgotten. He said, "Personality strengths must be watched as closely as personality weaknesses. A Christian who shows great compassion and mercy to others may at times reach too deeply and too far in trying to help another."

Good advice for those readers who may be saying, "Oh, that could never happen to me."

Short Wave Messages

Another beam sent out from God's lighthouse may come in the form of a "short-wave" message—or too many phone calls from the opposite sex.

I remember early in my Christian walk when a Christian male friend and I talked on the phone as much as three times a week. Our conversations were of the highest caliber spiritually, but he always called me from his office.

I enjoyed sharing with Bernie the wisdom and insight I gleaned from my conversations with this friend. I suppose this telephone relationship went on for about two years, mixed in with the few times we got together with him and his wife.

One day when he called, I was extremely busy and said, "Listen, could I call you back later this evening at home when I'm not as busy."

He hesitated and said, "No, I don't think so."

I stopped for a moment and then said, "Wait a minute. Doesn't your wife know that we talk on the phone all the time?" I had assumed all along that she did.

"No," he said. "She doesn't."

I knew right then that this telephone relationship must end. I could not imagine either of us being attracted to the other, but I saw that their marriage could be in jeopardy if his wife could not accept the regularity of his phone calls to me.

I'm grateful that in my naive state God warned me and gave me the good sense to cut off that kind of relationship immediately.

When someone other than your mate becomes your confidante—a friend's husband, the man at work or at church, or your next-door neighbor—take that as a clear warning sign that intimacy is starting outside of your marriage and CUT IT OFF!

Keeping a Safe Distance

When I was growing up, members of my extended family expressed themselves as an affectionate, touchy, huggy, kissy bunch. I'm still a toucher and love to express myself with my hands. I pat, console, and give approval physically as well as verbally.

But there are two instances when I get a check to hold back from hugging, touching, or kissing. One is if I feel particularly drawn to another man or if I suspect that he is particularly drawn to me.

Dr. Louis McBurney, founder of Marble Retreat Center in Marble, Colorado, said:

> Many innocent hugs show warmth and caring on a purely platonic level. You know the difference as well as I. But I'm very careful about touching some women, either because of signals from them or feelings of attraction within myself. Yet there are many others whom I can quite safely embrace.[3]

Have you heard the translation of K.I.S.S.? *Keep It Simple Stupid.* When a simple kiss and hug between you and your Christian brother changes from simply casual to wholly wonderful, that is your warning signal. Be on guard. The Holy Spirit will give you that "uh-uh" that something is getting out of control.

Sometimes it is not you who is being affected but the other person. I can best describe this again through my own experience. One afternoon I got a phone call from a dear friend. Bernie and I had been close friends with both him and his wife.

"Judy," he said, "this is Marvin." (Not his real name.)

"Hi, Marvin," I said. "Anything special?"

"Yes, Judy, there is. Would you mind if we stopped hugging?"

Time stopped for a moment as his words registered in my mind.

I simply blurted out, "Yes, that will be fine."

"Thank you," he replied and hung up the phone.

I don't know if you can imagine the shock I experienced. Here were two good friends and compatible communicators who had spoken less than two dozen words to each other and then hung up.

This is the classic example of how best to handle a situation. Marvin knew that he wanted to remain pure before God and pleasing to Him. I don't know how long he had been struggling with this problem—days—maybe weeks. But I know he felt sufficient in God's guidance to call, state one request, and hang up. There was no reason to say anything else.

Most people would have to explain and spew out details loading the other party with unnecessary knowledge, which may in turn worsen the matter by stirring up the other person.

When we hung up, I knelt before God and prayed for Marvin. Our friendship with him and his wife continued normally and uninterrupted.

Don't get out of balance on this and become cold and rigid around other Christians. Dr. Richard Dobbins expressed my feelings quite well:

> Fear of any physical contact with friends brings about an awkward isolation that is unwarranted. In wholesome friendships, a balance is sought between an isolation that is unwarranted and an intimacy that is unhealthy.[4]

If you will stay tuned in to God, He will alert you if that wholesome friendship begins to get out of balance.

Hidden Mine Fields

Sometimes a harbor may be loaded with hidden obstacles known only to the lighthouse master. Do you know what I consider to be a real source of trouble or a hidden time bomb in relationships other than marriage? It is when one person *gives a gift* in order to find a *special place in another's heart.*

One woman said, "Not long ago, I sent an evangelist friend of ours a small gift for his office—something for his desk that would remind him of me when he looked at it. The time and thought that went into purchasing this gift should have been a warning to me that I wanted a special place in his heart."

When we begin to invest emotional energy in another person, we have begun to "lay up treasures" in our heart. "For where your treasure is, there will your heart be also" (Luke 12:34). Some of us have rationalized that it is okay to romantically love two people simultaneously. This is not true! Jesus said we could not serve two masters. Eventually, we would love one and hate the other. As soon as we are aware that we are spending time and energy to please another, we must immediately redirect that energy back into the marriage relationship.

Another hidden time bomb may be uncovered when you find yourself *paying extra attention to your appearance* when in another's presence. One friend told me that other men often came to her house because of the nature of her husband's work. Occasionally, she would answer the door wearing slippers on her feet or rollers in her hair. But on the day that she knew a certain man dropped by for his report, she rose early, combed her hair, put on her makeup, and dressed as though she were going out for dinner.

Warning signs!

Maybe you recognize some of this in yourself. Are you becoming preoccupied in your thought life because of a special person? Have you ever driven your car from one place to another without remembering the route you took? Have you ever put clothes away without even remembering having removed them from the dryer or folded them because *he* was on your mind? If so, uncover these time bombs in prayer with God before they explode into reality.

Psalm 32 gives us an excellent prayer and promise for times like these. "*I acknowledged my sin* unto thee, and mine *iniquity have I not hid.* I said, I will *confess my transgressions* unto the Lord; and *thou forgavest* the iniquity of my sin" (Psalm 32:5, *italics added*).

Then, after praying that prayer, we can claim the following promise: "Thou art my hiding place; thou shalt preserve me from trouble; thou shalt compass me about with songs of deliverance" (Psalm 32:7).

Our Hiding Place

I cannot think of gaining any better "affair prevention" system than this one: God—my hiding place!

One woman who had attended one of my seminars wrote, "I am now aware of the warning signals that the Holy Spirit sends. By the grace of God, I can now respond to them instead of ignoring them. My eyes have been powerfully opened to view my own feelings and emotions, and, I realize that I do not have to succumb to them. No longer will I resist taking precaution. As a bonus, the Lord is gloriously restoring and returning to me my 'first love.' Your message has equipped me to effectively fight this battle and WIN!"

If you sense that your feelings for another are getting out of hand, take these warning signals seriously. A date with God has often prevented a date that you may be sorry later you had kept.

Principles for Prevention

"More is required than merely the effort to avoid lust and focus on godly desire. We must repent of the deeper issues that are feeding our lust. But one cannot deeply repent of what is unknown. We need to pray that God will reveal the secret things of our hearts" (Psalms 139).—Dan Allender[1]

Lust plays no favorites and has no barriers. Teenagers, single adults, and both happily and unhappily married have all fallen prey to this wicked devourer of souls.

In this chapter, I want to address the woman who has done some self-examination while reading these pages and recognizes some of the warning signals in herself. Now, in the early stages, is the time to adjust your armor and prepare for warfare. Before the enemy of your soul advances, you must guard your heart and shield your mind.

Be a 'Fraidy Cat

One of the best preventative measures against infidelity is to *fear the results of sin*. Become a 'fraidy' cat where sin is involved. Scare yourself by thinking of all the ramifications of your sinful choices before you go any further with your feelings. Think about others who have been unfaithful and what it has cost them, and relive those horror stories in your mind.

When asked what has kept him from immorality all these years, a friend replied in his inimitable way, "I'm afraid of God!"

Mark Twain once said, "The surest protection against temptation is cowardice." That's true, but not completely—God is the safest defense a Christian can have for affair prevention.

Now go back and think over all the Bible stories about unfaithfulness. Read Numbers 22–25 and see why 24,000 people died in one day. Read about David's sin with Bathsheba and the consequences— lies, murder, and the death of a child—not to mention the example David set for his own children. Absalom, David's beloved son, tried to rob the kingdom from his own father; and Amnon, another son, unable to control his lustful feelings, raped Tamar, his sister. How David's heart must have broken as he poured out his sorrow before God in Psalm 51.

Think of how much God has done for you and how much your sin would hurt Him. Then ask yourself this question . . . is it worth it to have "the pleasures of sin *for a season?*" (Hebrews 11:25, *italics added*).

Is it worth it to you to know that you gave part of yourself in a mystical union to someone other than whom God intended?

Is it worth it to you to see lives broken, marriages split, and children confused because your emotions have gotten out of hand?

Pastor Brian Harbour made this thought-provoking statement:

> Uncontrolled sex may bring pleasure for a moment, but it can bring tragedy for a lifetime. It will leave scars that will never be healed. It will lead to consequences that can never be undone. When you let sex get out of hand, it is going to bring difficulties into your life. You can count on it.[2]

How do you know when your feelings are getting out of hand?

Rodney Clapp said,

> When are feelings getting out of hand? When is innocent appreciation becoming out-and-out temptation? A good rule of thumb is that any feelings or actions that we are afraid to discuss with our spouse are probably dangerous.[3]

Repressing your feelings from your husband and friends will not save you from temptation. Most likely it will only increase your vulnerability. I've repeatedly given this advice: Talking this thing over with someone you know can help you through it. Don't go through it alone.

The first principle for affair prevention then is—be afraid, really afraid, of the mental anguish and slow death that sexual sin produces in a life. More people are stricken today with malignant tumors than they are by lightning. Adultery is like a malignant tumor—as it grows, it produces more and more suffering and then death.

Let Sleeping Dogs Lie

Another principle for prevention is to *deal with the need to finish old business*—such as memories of a former boyfriend. All too often when difficulties arise in a marriage, a woman may begin to think, I wonder what it would have been like if only. . . .

I know. I've done it. Before I met Bernie, I dated a fellow for over two years. We were both sure we would end up married to each other. I left for college and pledged my love to him. But while I was at college, I met my Robert Redford—Bernie (or so he was to me). I abruptly broke the relationship off with this other young man. I heard later that within three months after we had broken up, he married a widow with three children. I asked myself if that was a marriage on the rebound for which I had been responsible?

For years I condemned myself for the hurt I had caused him. When I committed my life to Jesus Christ, I began to pray for this man's salvation. It made me feel better to believe that if he could only come to know the love of God through Jesus Christ, it would make up for the hurt I had caused him. I thought maybe God would have me bump into him at an airport or in some other situation where I might speak to him concerning his salvation and free myself from the guilt.

But let me tell you how God removed this idea from my head.

A friend told me her story of trying to break ties with the memories of an old boyfriend. She wrote it down for me.

We broke up during our college years, but for me it was never really finished or resolved. Even after twenty-two years of marriage, I continued to think about him—especially during the difficult times.

I finally decided that I needed to get this thing out of my system. So I called him at his office and set up a time to see him. We had a pleasant visit and chit-chatted about old friends, and he invited me to come to his house to meet his family and have dinner with them.

When I went to their home, we had a lovely dinner, and then he took me on a tour of the house. When we got to his study, he opened a trunk and took out an old picture of me. His wife came in then and commented that she was glad I was taking the picture because he refused to get rid of it. All through the evening, I found he still had the same appeal to me as he had years ago. I was still sexually stimulated in his presence.

Later that evening, he drove me back to where I was staying. He said he wished that we could spend more time together so he could know who I really am now. I said that would be impossible for me because it would lead to sexual involvement, which I didn't want, and he said he didn't either.

Amid much tension and mixed emotion, we went our separate ways.

She concluded by telling me that if there were any way to handle the old boyfriend syndrome—that ain't it! She said it only fanned the flame of what she considered unfinished business. Her deliverance from her mental torment finally came after much communication and prayer for deliverance with her husband.

I had to see that a person who I loved long ago was a soul tie. Oh, how I loved to imagine we would meet once again. That is a soul tie. A sin. Share and confess your sin with another. Receive God's forgiveness to be cleansed. Ask, "*Why* did this soul tie happen?" Deal with your unfinished memories by refusing to allow them to live once again in your mind. Put them behind you. Bury them as God does your past sin, and get on with the work ordained for you today.

"Forgetting those things which are behind, and reaching forth unto those things which are before, I press toward the mark for the prize of the high calling of God in Christ Jesus" (Philippians 3:13–14).

On-the-Job Armor

What principle is available to you when your emotions get out of hand at your place of employment? This is a tough one because now you are in contact with this person on a day-to-day basis. But again we can go to God's Word for the principle of *putting on your full armor.*

When Potiphar's wife tempted Joseph, Scripture says, "And though she spoke to Joseph day after day, he refused to go to bed with her or even be with her" (Genesis 39:10, *NIV*). Daily temptation can easily wear one down if he/she is not prepared. Fortunately, Joseph was.

God has provided us with armor so we, like Joseph, may be strong in the face of "day-to-day" conflict.

Finally, my brethren, be strong in the Lord, and in the power of his might. Put on the whole armor of God, that ye may be able to stand against the wiles of the devil. For we wrestle not against flesh and blood, but against principalities, against powers, against the rulers of the darkness of this world, against spiritual wickedness in high places. Wherefore take unto you the whole armor of God, that ye may be able to withstand in the evil day, and having done all, to stand. Stand therefore, having your loins girt about with truth, and having on the breastplate of righteousness; and your feet shod with the preparation of the gospel of peace; above all, taking the shield of faith, wherewith ye shall be able to quench all the fiery darts of the wicked. And take the helmet of salvation, and the sword of the Spirit which is the word of God: Praying always with all prayer and supplication in the Spirit, and watching thereunto with all perseverance and supplication for all saints (Ephesians 6:10–18).

One married woman told me how she applied this verse to her situation. Prayer became her defensive armor. She said,

> I became very infatuated with my boss. He was fifteen years older than I and not really handsome. But he was charming, brilliant, witty, and he made me laugh. I realized I hadn't laughed in a long, long time. He was separated from his wife at the time. Many times during the day, I had to really pray hard, both in the Spirit and with my understanding, just as Scripture says. But I did overcome this infatuation through prayer because the Holy Spirit kept me and helped me.

A friend of mine who is a secretary to a pastor says she knows countless secretaries who have committed both mental and physical adultery with their spiritual employers. Here's one statement that should cause a woman to throw up her spiritual armor: "My wife doesn't understand me." Your response to this statement should be. "I'll pray for your marriage. In the meantime, why don't you seek some pastoral counseling." Do **not** counsel with him yourself. Instead, cover him with your prayers, and do not bring the subject up again.

Unfortunately, for some, the final answer may simply be to find another job and a boss who is more businesslike. No amount of benefits and wages is worth losing your husband, your family, or intimacy with God.

Another woman who became infatuated with a man at work told me she often asked her husband to meet her for lunch. When he would drop her off, she would give him a *big kiss* in front of everyone to remind them and herself where her emotions lay. Whenever she spoke of her marriage, she always gave the impression that she was the most happily married woman in the world.

This woman applied the principle of putting on her spiritual armor by girding herself with this truth: "Wives, submit yourselves unto your own husbands, as unto the Lord" (Ephesians 5:22). By putting on her breastplate of righteousness, she channeled her emotions back into her marriage, as should a virtuous woman.

Another practical way to apply a piece of armor may be by placing a picture of your husband on the corner of your desk at work. In fact, have a picture made for your husband's office, too, only make it a wall-sized one. That way whenever a "threat" walks into his office, she'll see you first glancing over his shoulder. You might even think about having a picture made with a shotgun in your hand. How's that for effectiveness?

Nip It in the Bud

Whether your source of sexual temptation is an old boyfriend, a man on the job, or only someone you have had a dream about, the solution is still the same. The greatest secret that I can share with women is this—your mind is your most important sex organ. Improper sexual behavior *always* starts first in the mind.

Charles Mylander said, "Win the battle with lust in your mind, and you will never fight it on the more lethal fronts of sinful actions or ingrained habits."[4]

Therefore, while this solution may sound simplistic—it is still the best answer: STOP THE THOUGHTS! Nip them in the bud. Bop them on the top. Do not let your imagination run away with you. Say "I quit that!" Say it again and again if you must.

Sometimes just standing at the checkout counter in a grocery store and looking at the title contents of the magazine in the racks can cause your imagination to run away. Just look somewhere else.

Choose not to review last night's passionate dream. Occupy your mind with organizing your day. Read the Bible, listen to a program on a Christian radio station, or dig out a new recipe for supper. Before long, the sexual thoughts will dissipate.

> I beseech you, therefore, brethren, by the mercies of God, that ye present your bodies a living sacrifice, holy, acceptable unto God, which is your reasonable service. And be not conformed to this world: but be ye transformed by the renewing of your mind, that ye may prove what is that good, and acceptable, and perfect, will of God"
> (Romans 12:1–2).

Remember my little motto, "Affairs start in the head before they get to the bed."

A friend told me this verse set her free. "Serve him with a perfect heart and with a willing mind; for the Lord searcheth all hearts, and understandeth all the imaginations of the thoughts" (1 Chronicles 28:9). She said, "Judy, I finally realized that God (who made me as I am) even knows what conjures up those thoughts. It occurred to me that God wouldn't keep such close tabs on my thoughts if He were only interested in my actions."

Don't rationalize or excuse yourself when you begin to entertain an impure thought. Deal with it immediately.

Sharpen Your Sword

The next principle for prevention of infidelity is one that I've woven throughout this book. I cannot emphasize enough *the importance of getting into the* **Word of God**. For a Christian, the Word of God is her sword and shield. "Sharper than any double-edged sword, it penetrates even to dividing soul and spirit, joints and marrow; it judges the thoughts and attitudes of the heart" (Hebrews 4:12, *NIV*).

God's Word can not only get you *out* of bondage, as we talked about in the previous chapter, but it can *keep* you from ever being placed in bondage. However, if you don't know what His Word says, how can you use it for your own protection?

For those having problems with sexual temptation, it may be a good idea to set some time apart for yourself daily just to sit in God's presence and read His Word regarding this subject. Recognizing your problem as, "I wanted something that didn't belong to me. I was discontent and wanted something more and that desire has driven me to immorality."

"You shall not covet your neighbor's house. You shall not covet your neighbor's wife, or his manservant or maidservant, his ox or donkey, or anything that belongs to your neighbor" (Exodus 20:17, *NIV*).

I have found the following verses to help you. As you read, you may want to mark them in your Bible for later reference.

Genesis 39:7–12	Romans 2:22
Exodus 20:14	Romans 13:9
Psalm 4:23	1 Corinthians 6:15–20
Proverbs 5	1 Corinthians 10:1–13
Proverbs 6:20–35	2 Corinthians 12:9
Proverbs 9:13–18	1 Thessalonians 4:1–8
Matthew 5:27; 19:18	1 John 5:4
Mark 10:19	James 1:13–16
John 17:15	James 2:11
Hebrews 2:18	

Back from the Brink

I want to share a bone-chilling experience I had. Let me use this story to illustrate God's power to keep us from going over the brink with the passions of the soul—in my case: fear of a mental breakdown.

Knowing God's Word and being able to allow it to completely fill my mind was the only way I could have possibly kept my sanity. My daughter Jill and I went to Seattle, Washington, to visit some old friends who had previously attended our church. Somehow the topic came up about climbing Mt. Rainier. The next day we left to climb the mountain before our vacation ended.

When the five of us started out that morning, I had no idea that I would soon be facing one of the most severe trials I had ever experienced. Our first warning came from the mountain ranger: "Don't go up the mountain without food or water; and do not, for any reason, leave the marked path." We had no water and no food other than a candy bar, and I was dressed in cotton clothing with only a light raincoat for protection.

The steepness of the climb required enormous effort on my part. I could barely breathe at times. By the time we had reached the snow line, we had climbed for almost three hours. We were tired, cold, and wet from the light rain and heavy fog that had settled upon the mountain.

At that point, I should have said, "Well, this has been great! Let's go back down now." But instead, Jill and her friend, Sean, decided that they wanted to get off the steep, treacherous trail, so they persuaded Sean's father to let them climb the rocky crags instead. Since Bob, Sean's father, was so positive they would be "just fine" and seemed to know much more about this mountain than I did, I reluctantly conceded.

In the meantime, we continued to climb. As we did, we met and spoke with several mountaineers passing us on their way down. "There's a blizzard at 11,000 feet with 40–50 mile an hour winds," they warned. Even the forest ranger came down. But we kept going.

If you can picture this in your mind, imagine the scene being laid out where I would soon be in the worst battle of my life—temptation to fall into bone-chilling fear and to fail to trust God in all things.

In spite of the cold, the fatigue, the warnings, and my growing fear, we continued to climb. Since our group had now been split, we could not make the decision to go down until we were all together. We had to keep going up, hoping they would be there when we arrived. Then a thought popped into my mind about several high school students who had recently lost their lives on a mountain climb at a nearby mountain because they got off the trail, got lost, and froze to death.

My fear rose with each step upward. Almost simultaneously, Bob and I shouted for Sean and Jill. There was no answer. Over and over we called. They should have been within hearing distance. Finally, Bob decided I should wait with Chad, his ten-year-old son, while he got off the trail to look for them—a dangerous idea in itself.

By now the fog was unbelievably thick, and I was soaking wet and shivering from the cold. I could hear Bob shouting in the distance but could hear no reply from Jill or Sean.

All this time, I was mentally casting my cares on the Lord and singing hymns, psalms, and spiritual songs in my heart. But fear escalated to near hysteria when I heard a monolithic rumble of rocks, which shouted, in my mind AVALANCHE!

Now the trial rolled into high gear. I began shouting, screaming, and hallucinating as nausea and panic overwhelmed me. I doubted that God had heard my prayers and wondered if there really was a God. The battle raged for my sanity and my faith as I mentally saw the headlines in tomorrow's newspaper: "CLIMBERS FOUND DEAD ON MT. RAINIER."

What kept me from hurling myself off the cliff to end the intensity of the battle? I finally got quiet before the Lord on that magnificent mountain and began to meditate on His Word. Verses came to my mind such as "I will never leave you nor forsake you" (Hebrews 13:5). Sometimes I spoke aloud or even shouted the verses that I had hidden in my heart. It did not occur to me to rationalize my emotions or tell myself to calm down. God knew I was beyond rational thinking. I simply centered my thinking upon Him and His Word: "For God hath not given us the spirit of fear; but of power, and of love, and of a sound mind" (2 Timothy 1:7). Slowly, comfort and strength began to replace hysteria.

Yes, there is a happy ending. About an hour later, Jill and Sean were found and finally returned to where we waited. I embraced my daughter with wondrous joy and thanksgiving to God—and my mind was still intact!

What *prevented* me from going over "the cliff" in the moments of tremendous emotional stress? God—and God alone. As I was experiencing this "trying out God to see if He is there" on the mountain, I thought of those who are also under tremendous stress and feel that "going over the cliff" or "giving in to the strong imaginings or passions" would be the best and easiest solution.

I was "losing it" on Mt. Rainier because of fear. You might find yourself losing it on the mountain of morality as lust shoves its way to the forefront. Whether it's fear, lust, or whatever, His grace, His Word, His outstretched arms are sufficient. The God kind of faith says, "I know He is real; He is a person; 'I am that I am' is there." This God has prevented multitudes from jumping off cliffs and multitudes more from jumping into immorality. Turn around and face Him.

Beyond any doubt, I know that God can and will come to our assistance in the midst of trial and temptation—whether it is the temptation not to trust God or the powerful temptation to commit adultery.

Finding Peace in a War-Zone

One night Bernie and I bought a pizza and sat down to talk about this message. I asked him how he handled temptation since becoming a believer in Christ. Without a bit of hesitation, he replied, "I apply Philippians 4:8 to my thoughts."

> Whatever is true, whatever is noble, whatever is right, whatever is pure, whatever is lovely, whatever is admirable—if anything is excellent or praiseworthy—think about such things. . . . And the God of peace will be with you (*NIV*).

Bernie knew that verse is the killer of ungodly thoughts.

"Impure thoughts must be redirected. You can't defeat impure thoughts by praying that they'll go away. That will just make you more obsessed with them," says Archibald Hart.

Good training influences you forever. And I'm convinced that training in God's Word will forever keep those earthly lusts at bay. The Greeks had a saying that moral strength was gained only by effort and self-control. To make a point, let me illustrate this way.

Not many people jogged, did aerobic exercises, or watched their fat and cholesterol intake until the American Medical Association issued repeated warnings that women as well as men were fast succumbing to heart disease. But through training and information, we are on the road to better health habits. And perhaps in a few years, because we have heeded this advice, we will see fewer and fewer deaths occur because of heart disease.

In like manner, God's Word can prevent the death brought about from immorality if we will only heed the information and tone up our spiritual and moral muscles.

One set of statistics has shown that out of 70,000 pilgrims in early America only six divorces occurred. During the colonial period, one out of every 500 marriages ended in divorce. By 1812, divorce hit one out of 110 marriages. In 1961, one out of every 3.7 marriages was affected. Today it is estimated that one out of every two marriages ends in divorce. We are indeed living in the midst of a battle for the home.

How does a marriage survive and a couple remain satisfied "till death do them part?" One of the best ways to find peace of mind and peace of heart is to do what Paul says. ". . . for I have learned, in whatsoever state I am, therewith to be content" (Philippians 4:11, *NIV*).

Repeatedly throughout this book we have examined the fact that a perfect mate and a perfect marriage do not exist. No one on earth will ever satisfy all our longings. Only God was meant to fill those empty places in our hearts.

As you work through these principles in prayer, Bible study, and by meditating on the Word, expect God to give you the rest, peace, and contentment that you so desire. Eventually, you will come to the place where you can say, "My soul, wait thou only upon God, for my expectation is from him" (Psalm 62:5).

9

How to Get Free When Your Feet Didn't Flee

"Few sins leave as many emotional scars as adultery. But a determined application of God's principles can lead to a new beginning."

—Timothy Santinga[1]

After having given you all the warnings and prevention principles, I know that for some of you this reading comes too late. This chapter was written for those women who are *now* involved in an adulterous situation or enslaved by any sexual ungodliness.

First and foremost, let me say there is a way out! It will be painful, but there is a way out! Breaking off a relationship where sexual intercourse has taken place will not be easy or emotionally pain-free. The Lord understands how difficult it is to let go of a relationship in which we are bound. But He also knows that, even though the pain is great, the cost to keep it is even greater.

God's Word tells us that a person has become a slave "to whatever has mastered him" (2 Peter 2:19, *NIV*). In other words, while you are involved in adultery, you are a slave—mastered by your situation, your feelings, and this other man. The only way your freedom will be won is by completely abolishing ownership.

Making a Decision

The first step you must take toward freedom and wholeness is not made in the bed but in your head. You must *choose* to free yourself from this sinful relationship. If you are a Christian, you *can* change. God said so.

"I can do all things through Christ which strengtheneth me" (Philippians 4:13).

To say, "I cannot change my situation or my feelings toward him" is not the truth. Rather it is a decision not to believe God. If this is your decision, you would be more honest to say, "I *will not* change." True, your feelings will not be changed overnight. And . . . you cannot change feelings by your will. Willpower will not set us free from the feelings that come from our unredeemed appetites. Only God can do that miracle. What you *do* change is your actions, which will immediately stop the immorality.

Feelings follow actions, and love is primarily an action of the will. Certainly, feelings, attraction, and desire are all part of two people wanting to spend their lives together. But feelings and circumstances change. What happens to a couple if disability or illness changes physical attraction?

Feelings will always follow what your will sets out to do. God's grace (His enablement) is in charge of that. It is a gradual happening, as most will testify.

Doctors Paul Meier and Frank Minirth wrote:

> As psychiatrists we cringe whenever (Christian) patients use the word can't. . . . "I can't" and "I've tried" are merely lame excuses. . . . If an individual changes all his can'ts to won'ts, he stops avoiding the truth, quits deceiving himself, and starts living in reality.[2]

For those now involved in an affair let me say that the *I can't change* and the *I won't change* attitudes both lead to death, but one answer is deceitful and the other truthful.

Do you feel shame? Do you know that what you have been doing is wrong, impure, and unclean? Do you know that your sin has broken God's heart? Do you know that because of this affair you are cut off from God's presence?

"But your iniquities have separated you from your God; your sins have hid *his* face from you, that he will not hear" (Isaiah 59:2).

Exchanging Darkness for Light

All the information in this chapter will be of no avail and will fall on deaf ears if you do not first depend on the mystical power of our very real God who will, on your behalf, cleanse you. Confession, cleansing, and repentance are the essential catalysts for change.

Look again at the passage in Ephesians 5:13–14. "But everything exposed by the light becomes visible, for it is light that makes everything visible. This is why it is said: 'Wake up, O sleeper, rise from the dead, and Christ will shine on you' " (*NIV*). What this means is that your secret, although dark, can be translated into light when God is allowed access into your abyss!

"For God, who commanded the light to shine out of darkness, hath shined in our hearts, to give the light of the knowledge of the glory of God in the face of Jesus Christ" (2 Corinthians 4:6).

Jesus Christ came to earth to light the path that sinners may once again find their way back to God. He said to the Pharisees, "I came not to call the righteous, but sinners to repentance" (Luke 5:32).

To repent means to confess the wrong you have done and to turn completely away from this wrong. Repentance means more than simply feeling bad as a result of your actions. Remorse or embarrassment may be felt simply because infidelity has been discovered by others. For instance, a person may go to God in prayer and say, "I'm so sorry, and I wish I had not done that." But the underlying motive in her heart is, "I'm sorry because, more than anything, I don't want anyone to find out what I have done." This person's motive in going to God originates out of pride rather than out of humility.

But godly sorrow, which leads to repentance, comes from the Holy Spirit who was sent by God to "reprove the world of sin" (John 16:8). Godly sorrow means your sin is as ugly to you as it is to God, and you are willing to stop sinning and *completely change.* Then God forgives and *forgets.* He will never revoke? His pardon and will treat the sin as if He had forgotten it. "For I will forgive their wickedness and will remember their sins no more" (Hebrews 8:12, *NIV*).

Why not stop now and pray this prayer:

Father, how I appreciate your magnificent insights into my heart. Because You see so clearly and so perfectly, You are able to speak with clarity in the midst of my confusion, hurt, and sin. You and You alone fully know me.

Where can I go to find meaning in life except to You?

I fully turn around to face You just as I am. Here, Lord, are my inadequacies and my enslavements to sin staring at You. Greater than any laser is Your power on my behalf to split open this bondage. I'm so thankful for that.

I've been so wrong Father, and You have been so right in Your assessment of what I've been doing. Give me the spirit of godly repentance so that I may be free—free to worship and praise You.

Forgive me, God, and make me whole and pure before You. I bow before You and inwardly accept this cleansing and forgiveness by faith. Wash me with the blood of Jesus, who gave me a way to be set free from these sins.

Transform me in this situation. I don't want to escape from the reality of it anymore.

May Your love wash over me daily. I want to walk with You. I depend on Your mercy and grace, and I choose to obey Your directives as I flee from my own immorality.

Thank You, God, for so great a salvation and for giving me a freshly washed countenance that I may look at You unashamedly. In Jesus' name. Amen.

Forgiving Ourselves

Once we have given our sins to God and received His forgiveness, we often find another parasite gnawing at our souls. It is the inability to forgive ourselves. Paul said, ". . . *this* one thing I *do,* forgetting those things which are behind, and reaching forth unto those things which are before, I press toward the mark for the prize of the high calling of God in Christ Jesus" (Philippians 3:13–14).

If you refuse to forgive yourself, even though God has, then you have made yourself a fourth member of the Trinity—and that is an impossibility. God alone sits on the throne of judgment. When God forgives us, we must either agree or disagree with Him.

Perhaps self-hatred lingers longest after committing the sin of infidelity because the Bible tells us, "All other sins a man commits are outside his body, but he who sins sexually sins against his own body" (1 Corinthians 6:18, *NIV*). Intuitively, our spirit knows, even if our conscious minds do not understand, that we have given a part of ourselves to another, affronting our delicate psyche.

Often our problem lies in *forgetting* rather than forgiving.

Jay Adams, noted author and Christian counselor, said, "Forgiveness does not mean necessarily forgetting immediately, but it does involve a commitment not to raise the issue again."

God said, "I will forgive their iniquity, and I will remember their sin no more" (Jeremiah 31:34). God has willed to forgive and forget. So must we! In order to forgive ourselves, we must take action against any thought that may lead us back to bondage. Replacing ungodly thoughts with godly thoughts, and directing and renewing your mind are all paths to the road called freedom.

When condemnation comes, you must not entertain it, dwell on it, or in any way play out the scenario of your sin in your mind. Use that phrase I gave you earlier in the book, "I quit that!" What a relief it is to see yourself cleansed as God does. Once again you are fresh, whole, and complete in Him. When you have dealt with the truth of God's Word, you are now responsible to tell your feelings to fall in line with the facts. God has forgiven you, and there is nothing more to say!

Calling All Troops

When you have made a decision to allow God to work in your heart and in your situation, help is on the way. But let me warn you, you may be in for one of the fiercest spiritual battles you have ever fought. Satan knows your lack of moral strength from the past. He will do everything in his power to keep you in darkness. Remember that "God is faithful, he will not let you be tempted beyond what you can bear. But when you are tempted, he will also provide a way out so that you can stand up under it" (1 Corinthians 10:13, *NIV*).

Wars are not fought by single soldiers. Armies are sent to win the victory. So you, too, must call on your army of helpers, both heavenly and earthly, to come to your aid.

"Where no counsel is, the people fall: but in the multitude of counselors there is safety" (Proverbs 11:14).

Your frontline attack is the cross of Christ. In Exodus, chapter seventeen, Moses led the battle against the Amalekites. He stood before his enemy with the rod in his uplifted hand. As long as the rod was held up, the Israelites prevailed in battle. But when Moses' hands would fall from fatigue, the victory shifted to the enemy. So Aaron, his brother, and Hur the son of Caleb got on either side of him to support him.

"But Moses' hands were heavy; and they took a stone, and put it under him, and he sat thereon; and Aaron and Hur stayed up his hands, the one on the one side, and the other on the other side; and his hands were steady until the going down of the sun. And Joshua discomfited Amalek and his people with the edge of the sword" (Exodus 17:12–13).

The principle here is that when your battle becomes fierce, keep the cross (what Jesus Christ accomplished for us at Calvary—freedom from the power of sin in this case) before you.

If you become weary and drop your guard or see your enemy advancing, sit down and allow your Aaron or Hur to support your hands. Open up to one or two spiritual helpers who will support you. Let them know you are not double-minded and that you desire to be completely healed. You must have help in the beginning. "Confess your faults one to another, and pray one for another, that ye may be healed" (James 5:16).

A word of precaution is in order here. Each person's story and/or husband is unique. If you know this confession will be too difficult for your husband to handle, then seek the help of your pastor. God must tell you *if* and *when* you are to go to your husband.

Many years ago a well-meaning evangelist commanded the women in his audience to go home and confess to their husbands their past sexual sins—abortion, adultery, and whatever else they could think of. And they did! For weeks to follow, church counseling centers buzzed with more activity than they could handle. Unfortunately, many who came for counseling ended up in the divorce court. The Lord must individually lead us according to His knowledge and timing.

"He leadeth me in the paths of righteousness for his name's sake" (Psalm 23:3).

During this time, you may also want to ask your supporters to commit themselves to you to be available to talk, to seek God for wisdom and knowledge, and to intercede in prayer.

No one need battle alone. I know women who are leading double lives, racked in the torment of being married to one and having affection toward the other, but who will allow no one to go to battle with them. Unfortunately, they have deceived themselves, and the battle rages.

Run, Run, Get Away

Up to this point I've given you specific help in the spiritual department. Now I want to discuss a physical action you must take to free yourself. Three specific verses in the Bible tell us how.

1. "*Flee* fornication. Every sin that a man doeth is without the body; but he that committeth fornication sinneth against his own body" (1 Corinthians 6:18, *italics added*).

In the book *Marriage, Divorce and Remarriage in the Bible,* Jay Adams clearly defines fornication. "Fornication refers to sexual sin of any and all sorts. . . . fornication covers incest, bestiality, homosexuality and lesbianism as well as adultery."[3]

2. "Wherefore, my dearly beloved, *flee* from idolatry" (1 Corinthians 10:14, *italics added*).

3. "Flee also youthful lusts" (2 Timothy 2:22, italics added). Flee means move swiftly—vanish. Don't stand there and resist—"run away, Amigo!" What does Scripture mean when it tells us to flee from these three—fornication, idolatry, and youthful lusts?

It means—CUT IT OFF, PLUCK IT OUT, HANG IT UP!

Now that repentance, forgiveness, and cleansing have occurred in your life, you must deal with this man with whom you were involved. One initial form of communication should take place between you and him. "It is over. I have repented and have turned back to God." Any other similar, short conversation is appropriate. No long talks, no long explanations, no secret meeting places arranged to iron it all out, no parting tears of sweet sorrow. God said, "PLUCK and CUT!"

Then don't answer the phone when he calls, don't answer the door if he comes by, and don't reply to notes or letters you receive. FINISHED MEANS FINISHED.

Don't feel sorry for him or worry about him. You must see him as an enemy agent sent to destroy your life. Period! A few well-chosen words and then goodbye—otherwise you will have given Satan a handle to keep tugging at your heart.

Removing the Props

One of the most breathtaking sights I have ever seen is Macy's window at Christmas. The designs are a fascinating, artistic, winter wonderland. I would like to pretend I'm in one of those window scenes, rather than standing on the busy streets of New York City.

But once the holidays are over, every fragile mannequin, toy, and snowflake must be removed. When Easter rolls around, a whole new set of props is skillfully placed in the giant windows, and not one snowflake can be found mixed in with the Easter eggs.

Sexual sin is like experiencing winter in your life—a nuclear winter if you will. While some scenes seem beautiful, the overall reality is long, bleak months filled with ice, snow, and darkened days.

But when you have put your winter season of sin behind you, it is time for you, also, to change your props. "The old has gone, the new has come" (2 Corinthians 5:17, *NIV*).

Every letter, gift, photo, tape, video, email (!)—everything that was once a part of your illicit relationship must be chucked. Don't keep those letters tied with a red ribbon tucked away in the back of a drawer. Until you rid yourself of all sentiments and remembrances of the past, nostalgia will come creeping in upon you when you happen upon these old props. There will be enough mental remembrances that you will have to deal with without having physical reminders also.

Your Easter of resurrected life has come. Blow off every snowflake that wants to stick.

"Put ye on the Lord Jesus Christ, and make not provision for the flesh, to fulfill the lusts thereof" (Romans 13:14).

Tell Yourself the Truth

Once this drastic action of separation from him and his remembrances has taken place, invite yourself out to lunch, sit down, and have a good, long chat with yourself.

God told us that we must come from darkness to light by renewing our mind. So start telling yourself the *truth*. You were on the road to death and destruction, but by God's grace and forgiveness you are now on the road to life and wholeness.

When Jesus did battle with Satan, He did it with God's Word. So, you, too, would do well to fill your heart and mind with Scripture daily. And when the tempter comes to tell you what a glorious time you are missing because you are not with that other person, TELL HIM AND YOURSELF WHAT GOD SAYS!

James Beale, a Michigan pastor, gave an unforgettable message at a conference a few years ago on sovereignty and ownership. He said that Joseph had an absolute understanding regarding ownership. Joseph refused Potiphar's wife and said to her, "Because you are *his* wife" (Genesis 39:9, *NIV, italics added*). He kept himself where he belonged. God, in His sovereignty, tells us what we can and can't touch.

Pastor Beale said that when God put the marvelous tree of knowledge of good and evil in the garden, man desired to have it when he looked at it. But God also gave the tremendous power of decision. There is no self-control without our personal decision to exercise it. We exercise self-control not because we are afraid of being found out, but because it is a matter of personal choice. We keep ourselves from the forbidden tree because God commanded it, and we desire to obey Him.

According to Pastor Beale, there is nothing more nonsensical in God's world than getting hung up in adultery. "Someone else's partner is off-limits to us. That is something you don't think about, you don't touch, and you get out of your head. THAT TREE IS OFF-LIMITS. God said it, and that's all there is to it."

Tell yourself these things every time you are tempted to have one more look at that magnificent tree. Talk to yourself about ownership, and remember who you belong to—your husband.

I recently heard this story about how St. Augustine dealt with a person from his unregenerate past. After he had been converted, he met a woman on the street with whom he had been in sin's bondage. He passed her with a simple nod; but she stopped him and said, "Augustine! Don't you recognize me any more? It is I."

He looked at her intently for a moment, knowing that she no longer had the power to keep him under her evil spell. Then he responded, "Ah, but it is not I."

When sin comes knocking at your door, looking for our unregenerate self, we, too, may respond, "Sorry, the old me doesn't live here any more."

> I am crucified with Christ; nevertheless I live; yet not I, but Christ liveth in me; and the life which I now live in the flesh I live by the faith of the Son of God, who loved me, and gave himself for me (Galatians 2:20).

10

Walking in Freedom

"We are half-hearted creatures fooling about
with drink and sex and ambition when infinite joy is
offered us, like an ignorant child who wants to go on
making mud pies in a slum because he cannot
imagine what is meant by the offer of a holiday at
the sea. We are far too easily pleased."—C. S. Lewis[1]

Let's explore the different ways a woman, once
bound in sexual sin, can stay free and pure while
living in a world that is not. I wish I could sit down
with you, share a cup of tea, and pour out my heart
over what it has cost in this season of my life to write
this book. I don't want to be known as the Dr. Ruth of
Christendom, as some of my friends have teasingly
called me. Yet, I see too many Christians choking on
their own lust-filled problems for me to ignore this
issue.

The stories of broken lives, ruined by adulterous affairs, kept coming to me even as I typed the final
words. I'm full of grief when I hear how an act of sex,
which God created for pleasure and procreation,
became a playground for the devil. Illicit sex has
destroyed the virginity of the young, caused abortions,

destroyed the hearts and minds of spouses and their children, and brought mysterious diseases to the forefront. More fearsome than that, though, is the knowledge that God's judgment will and must fall on this immorality.

I believe the majority of you have had an occasional struggle with lust—enough so to purchase this book. Buying this book should have been more than an interesting investment; it should have been a *transforming* experience.

In the beginning I said I would write an "affair prevention" book. I have offered you no easy *formulas.* There are none. Many will say *they* have the *only* formula to free you from sin's bondage. While those formulas may work for them, for others, they will not.

My concern is that, once you are free, will you be able to "stand fast . . . in the liberty wherewith Christ hath made us free, and be not entangled again with the yoke of bondage" (Galatians 5:1).

Centered on Christ Alone

Staying *centered* on the work that Christ has done for us, on the cross and in His resurrection, will bring the promised freedom from sin. Because I think this truth is the one with the most scriptural foundation, it is the one I recommend.

Christ is our Deliverer. Christ—and Christ alone.

I'm grateful for the amount of in-depth counseling going on in the church today because many are being helped on their road to maturity.

However, I'm concerned over the high percentage of those counseled who continue to look to their counselors for all the answers. They have become *dependent* on receiving help through human assistance. If this were the way God meant us to go, the Bible would be full of instructions on "how to psychoanalyze from a Christian perspective."

That is not what the apostle Paul tells us. He emphasized Jesus, what He did, and how His redemptive work applies to our release from the slavery of sin.

In exceptional cases, however, mature spiritual help from a qualified pastor or counselor is absolutely necessary when vice-like demonic enslavement exists. When a person has been involved with perversion such as incest, lesbianism, child molestation, pornography, fantasizing with accompanying orgasms, or unwarranted sexual fear—then deliverance may be the answer. Such cases are, however, in the minority. The majority of problems stem from an inability to mortify the fleshly appetites and/or unwillingness to receive God's grace in the temptation and live with self-control.

Once counselors have helped people become set free from their sin, then they must also teach them how to receive direct help from God in order to stay free.

In addition, I would mention briefly that a woman may save herself much grief from demonic oppression by forgiving past family sexual sin. Many who have refused to forgive parents or grandparents for sexual sin have hardened themselves and become insensitive to God. In doing so, they have actually opened the door to sexual sin in their own life. Forgive your ancestors. The cost to your soul is too great not to.

Little by Little

To understand deliverance from sin, we must know God's ways. Some have told me, "I cried out to God, and He delivered me *immediately* from all my fears." Others have asked, "Why does God answer my prayer on the 100th time instead of the 99th?" I don't know. God is God. Since His wisdom is far greater than ours, we can trust that whatever He is working out in our lives is for our good and for His glory.

J. I. Packer writes these lines giving us some insight into God's ways.

> Perhaps He means to strengthen us in patience, good humor, compassion, humility, or meekness, by giving us some extra practice in exercising these graces under specially difficult conditions. Perhaps He has new lessons in self-denial and self-distrust to teach us. Perhaps He wishes to break us of complacency, or unreality, or undetected forms of pride and conceit. Perhaps His purpose is simply to draw us closer to Himself in conscious communion with Him; for it is often the case, as all the saints know, that fellowship with the Father and the Son is most vivid and sweet, and Christian joy is greatest, when the cross is the heaviest. . . . Or perhaps God is preparing us for forms of service of which at present we have no inkling.[2]

Sometimes God delivers immediately, but not always. I have received His help both ways. When I first became a Christian, He delivered me immediately from smoking and TV addiction and healed me of eczema. God just lifted them all from me. I thought, "What a life this will be from now on! Easy Street has arrived. If I ever make a mistake, I'll just go to God and be instantly delivered from all my plaguing emotions and trials." My, oh my, was I wrong.

God shed some light into my life as I read how He sent deliverance and help to His troubled people.

> I will send my fear before thee, and will destroy all the people to whom thou shalt come, and I will make all thine enemies turn their backs unto

thee. And I will send hornets before thee, which shall drive out the Hivite, the Canaanite, and the Hittite, from before thee. I will not drive them out from before thee in one year; lest the land *become desolate, and the beast of the field multiply against thee. By little* and little I will drive them out from before thee, until thou be increased, and inherit the land (Exodus 23:27–31, *italics added*).

Little by little? No, God, I thought. Why don't You deliver everyone who loves You from their fleshly sins all at one time? The flesh is an enemy to our spirit. Let's be done with it—the taste of it, the temptation of it, the repeat of its forces—so we can walk in victory and glory. After all, didn't the walls of Jericho come down immediately? That's the way I want deliverance from my sins, too, God.

But most of my victories have come, instead, through God's little-by-little method, flanked on one side by the *Lord's grace* and on the other with *my own self-control and dogged determination* to overcome.

Many women who have opened up to me about their problems with lust draw a mental picture of a battlefield. It seems unfitting that we, precious brides of Christ, should have combat boots on as we walk the aisle of life toward meeting our Husband.

Little by little, however, as we possess our land, the enemy will retreat. Although he may stagger around on your field of life, he will become powerless to reinstate himself in the trenches of your soul ever again—if you so choose. "Let not sin therefore reign in your mortal body that ye should obey it in the lusts thereof" (Romans 6:12).

Growing up in a Jewish home, I looked forward to the celebration of Chanukah. Traditionally, each child in the family received one gift for eight consecutive nights. Each night the children received a more meaningful gift. The time that elapsed between gifts made me appreciate each one individually. My parents would tell us where and why they selected that particular gift and why it was special. By the end of the week, I truly appreciated what my parents had done for me.

When I became a Christian, however, Christmas morning gift-giving replaced the eight-day tradition. Our four little children pounced on the myriad of packages, massacred the wrappings, and pummeled the boxes. In fifteen minutes they had jumped from one gift to the other, hardly noticing what they had opened. They did not appreciate the time or energy we spent in picking out their gifts. This reminds me again of Exodus 23 and "little by little."

God used much wisdom in not giving the whole land at once to His children. It would have been too much, too soon. In their lack of appreciation and immaturity, their land would have become desolate, and "the beast of the field" would have multiplied against them.

To you who have been forgiven of your sexual sin and sincerely desire holiness but still hear the echoing memories and still experience unclean desires, be patient. Sometimes it is God's way to deliver you from sin's last dregs little by little.

I do not mean to imply that this is His standard way for all of you struggling with immoral thoughts and deeds. But for those whom God chooses to deliver in this way, continue to walk with Him, trusting Him that each step in faith and each cry unto God will bring you closer to possessing lifelong freedom from that last drop of specific sin.

That truth comes not from what others have told me but from my own experiential knowledge of the "line upon line" mortification of my own unique sins of the flesh.

Look to the Cross

I enjoy standing on the water's edge looking out into the Gulf of Mexico. The emerald clear ocean shaded by the gigantic billows of blue clouds inspires me. When I yearn for beauty, simplicity, and solitude, nothing surpasses the sugar-white sands of northwest Florida.

But take me into the woods, and I have a different story to tell. In spite of the beauty of the greenery and the sun's rays streaking through the leaves, I get caught up in watching for snakes, poison ivy, and insects. I prefer the simplicity of the ocean rather than a bothersome walk through the woods.

Some of you have never stood on the sugar-white sand and seen the tranquility of the Gulf. You only know about it from what I've told you. The key to living, however, is to experience something for yourself.

Envision Mary actually standing by mankind's pivotal event. *She* was THERE experiencing the eternal effect of the crucifixion moment. No one could ever change her mind about what she saw at the foot of Calvary. What took place between Jesus and the Father could never be denied.

Mary also experienced seeing the stone rolled away at the tomb and seeing only burial clothes where once a dead body lay. But the disciples were filled with anxiety. Until they, too, had experienced firsthand the resurrected Christ, Mary's message of peace was only a story. They had to experience for themselves the same things that Mary had.

Without a revelation of Calvary, we will surely hop from one method to another in order to stay free. But once you grasp what Christ has accomplished for you, you will rarely have to seek counseling or run to the bookstore for one more book of *helps.* You will be able to live out who you are in Christ.

This is why I prefer to direct this chapter on staying free to the simplicity of Jesus' death and resurrection rather than on any other suggested "key to life." How sweet to have the knowledge that Christ has won the victory for us. When we fall down or when we forget, we need to get up and remember that we can find rest and solitude on the sugar-white sands of our salvation.

I do appreciate and thank God for all the teachers and counselors who, through their peek into the Word, have caught a glimpse of the truth and have ministered that truth. But the entire truth has been summed up in the heartbeat of Paul's soul:

> I am determined not to know any thing among you, save Jesus Christ, and him crucified (1 Corinthians 2:2).

> God forbid that I should glory, save in the cross of our Lord Jesus Christ (Galatians 6:14).

This truth has cut through the mountains of books, tapes, and teachings in my search for victory over the obstinate shoving of my unredeemed flesh.

Jesus Christ has provided everything— EVERYTHING—we will ever need to keep us free from the bondage of sin and condemnation.

When Israel looked to other "gods" to deliver them, God sent a prophet to plead with them to stop and see who God is. God's message was that it is madness to search for help anywhere but in Him. God did not tell us there were no other "gods"—man can make a god out of anything he pleases—He told us we "shall have *no* other gods." (See Exodus 20:3)

Christ Who Lives in Me

In my years of maturing as a believer, one practice that has been my strongest weapon against wrong thinking has been this: "Christ in you, the hope of glory" (Colossians 1:27).

Hudson Taylor, missionary to China, had been a toiling, burdened worker for the Lord. He wrote the following letter to a friend, describing his inner struggle with sin.

> I cannot tell you how I am buffeted sometimes by temptation. I never knew how bad a heart I have. Yet I do know that I love God and love His work, and desire to serve Him only and in all things. And I value above all else that precious Savior in whom alone I can be accepted. Often I am tempted to think that one so full of sin cannot be a child of God at all. But I try to throw it back, and rejoice all the more in the preciousness of Jesus and in the riches of the grace that has made us "accepted in the Beloved" . . . But oh, how short I fall here again! May God help me to love Him more and serve Him better. Do pray for me. Pray that the Lord will keep me from sin.[3]

These were Hudson Taylor's days of darkness. But six months after he had written this letter, Taylor, enlightened and illumined by the Spirit of God, boarded a northbound junk on the Grand Canal to visit his friend in Yangchow. Scarcely waiting for greetings, Taylor plunged into his story with his friend, Mr. Judd.

"Oh, Mr. Judd, God has made me a new man! God has made me a new man! Whereas I was blind, now I see!"

We have not been told exactly how the miracle was wrought, but Mr. Judd recorded that Taylor had experienced an *exchanged life.*

"No longer do I live, Mr. Judd," Taylor said. "Christ liveth in me. Instead of bondage, there is liberty. Instead of failure, I have quiet victory within. Instead of fear and weakness, I have a restful sense of sufficiency in Another."

This exchanged life did not come by striving after faith but by realizing what Christ had done on the cross and by resting on the Faithful One.

In saying these things, I am not digressing from my subject of lust. But in this all-important section regarding staying free, I cannot address it without desiring for you to understand completely the meaning of the Cross!

I wholeheartedly recommend David Needham's book *Birthright.* It was while reading and studying this work that I, like Hudson Taylor, was radically changed, and joy and gratefulness filled my heart.

He Makes the Difference

Two passages from Scripture are important to help you apply the truth that Christ truly does live in you.

"For ye are dead [the old man], and your life [the new you] is hid with Christ in God" (Colossians 3:3). The old life has passed, and your new life is safely sealed in Christ's care.

When you are tempted to settle into old habits and patterns of obeying your emotions rather than God's Word, you can rely on Christ to help you "Walk in the Spirit, and ye shall not fulfill the lust of the flesh" (Galatians 5:16).

When I decided to take God at His Word and yield to this truth that Christ did, indeed, live in me,

God allowed a situation to occur where I could experience the reality of the living Christ.

I had been invited to minister in a western city. The host family with whom I was staying for the entire week shook me to my very foundations. I needed quiet rest and a still mind to formulate my daily messages, but I found just the opposite.

Each family member had deep personality disorders that manifested when they were all together. They insulted each other continually. One member was a drug user, one a religious reprobate, one an unwed suicidal mother, and my hostess—the mother of them all. The husband had been a pastor who, years before, had left the ministry in bitterness.

Unable to concentrate, I was sure I would not last the week in this home. In my flesh, a brilliant plan came to my mind. Rather than associate with these people, I decided to hibernate in my room and fast all week. Then I would not have to face the difficulties and conflicts that existed in this home. Withdrawal was my usual means of escaping unpleasantries.

But this week had come only one week after I fully believed God that "it is no longer I who lives but Christ who lives in me." Now I was in a crisis. I paced the bedroom floor reminding myself of this newly-understood truth. I told myself who God was and that I belonged to Him. I meditated on His character with all my faculties. But when I thought of going back downstairs with these people, my throat tightened up, and I felt woozy and nauseated. Satan did not want me to experience the reality of Christ living through me.

I prayed, "C'mon God. Push through these human emotions. I bow before You. I yield my nervousness to You, my anger toward this problem, and my disgust with this family. I'll keep concentrating on Your Word until I am able to go down those steps and eat dinner like the new person You made me to be. I'm in You, God, and You are in me!"

That week stands out as a beacon in my Christian experience. As I look back, I can hardly believe how mightily God manifested Himself through me. I ate dinner every night with that family and was able to share Christ's love. The former pastor allowed me to counsel with him and pray with his family. I could never have done this unless Christ lived in me and I in Him.

> For they that are after the flesh do mind the things of the flesh; but they that are after the Spirit, the things of the Spirit. For to be carnally minded is death; but to be spiritually minded is life and peace (Romans 8:5–6).

> Set your affection on things above, not on things on the earth. For ye are dead, and your life is hid with Christ in God (Colossians 3:2–3).

In the area of sexual temptation, everything I have just written will be God's saving grace for you to get free and stay free. If you set your mind according to what you see and hear in the worldly realm, your emotions will follow. It is impossible to get rid of your thoughts by sheer self-will. You cannot tell your emotions or your glands to stop. They will not listen to you.

Choosing, however, to allow Christ to control these emotions, will indeed bring the ultimate and final victory to your situation. There is no formula to follow. During my battles, I have cried "C'mon, God!" thousands of times as I practice the yielding of my flesh to the Spirit within me. You must in every situation exchange your habits, your wisdom, and your actions for His perfect ways. You can choose your ultimate fate.

"Put ye on the Lord Jesus Christ, and make not provision for the flesh, to fulfill the lusts thereof" (Romans 13:14).

Self-Control Versus Self-Discipline

I haven't used the word self-discipline as an operative word in this chapter. I like to use the word self-control instead. What is the difference?

Outwardly watching two women walk in morality, resisting infatuation, will not enable us to determine whether they are behaving rightly as a result of self-*discipline* or self-*control*. How would you be able to determine the difference? Is one of the ways a new and living way in Christ Jesus? Does one of the ways make God smile? I believe so.

It is the *motive* behind their behavior that would let us know whether a person is exercising self-discipline or self-control. Of course damaging urges need to be controlled. But, **why** do we control them?

With this issue of morality, both women would think, "I will not go any further with this man in a relationship."

With this in mind, let's listen to what the one who is given to **self-discipline** may be thinking:

> I know this is wrong for me to want, but sexually (my unredeemed appetite), I still desire to sin. I want relief. I want pleasure. Life is hard. I want something in return. But, I shouldn't be walking in immorality. God is giving me a strong NO—so I won't. **I must** control the bad. **I must** try harder. **I must** stop those the things **I want** to do. **I want** to feel good about myself so I must follow . . . *these rules I've set up for myself.*

The person who is given to **self-control** is thinking:

I know this is wrong for me to want, but sexually (my unredeemed appetite), I still desire to sin. I want relief. I want pleasure. Life is hard. I want something in return. But, I shouldn't be walking in immorality. God is giving me a strong NO. I struggle in my walk between my flesh and my spirit, yet I know my genuine life comes from and is united with God. Therefore, I am free to operate in a new way to live in righteousness. The only way for the Spirit to work in me and through me is for me to not deny my helplessness, my repeated failures in certain areas of life. I choose to embrace what is true about myself in those areas . . . I just can't get it right! Lord, I give up.

I do not want to use my energy to set up disciplines that bring me into bondage once again. Rather, I exercise *self-control* as one who, in my deepest part, desires to know God. To know God is to acknowledge that even my resisting sin has to do with **His** empowerment through my newly created spirit man, as opposed to my old focus of severity toward my behavior. I want to exercise my spiritual senses by drinking from this new well of freedom.

Yet, if you know at times you can't find inside you anything that wants to "stay out of trouble" (our maturity isn't full yet!) then just choose to obey by *self-discipline.* I like the way author Larry Crabb explained it in an interview, "If the best I can do in my own spiritual maturity is to exercise self-discipline and to make the choice not to go [to the adult bookstore] because the Bible is clear on the topic, then I would say it is fine [to obey out of self-discipline]. That, to me, is a huge difference."

But, he fully advocates self-control over self-discipline saying that there is still effort involved, but it isn't compulsive and strenuous like self-discipline is. Repression focuses on controlling the bad and self-control focuses on pursuing good.

11

The Choice is Yours

"The greatest accuser of the person with a broken world is the broken-world person himself. With alarming frequency the circuitry of accusation activated somewhere deep within. It would replay the past and remind me of past feelings: cheapness, failure, wreckage. There was no way back, the 'accuser' would say. But then a stronger voice would emerge from the deep and say: Either you believe in the capacity of Christ's atonement to make you a new person or you don't. If you do, then start living like a forgiven person should live."—Gordon MacDonald[1]

Before I came to this point in the book, I profited by the Bible teaching of a well-known woman. I held her in high esteem, read all of her books, and sought to model my walk after hers. Then I heard that this spiritual giant of a woman had fallen into sexual sin. I was shattered. For days I reeled, wondering, after all this research and writing, what I could possibly say that this woman did not know: and yet, she fell.

After three days of moping about the house thinking and praying about this, I believe God gave me the answer. Even though each believer is unique and has different gifts and ministries, we all have been given the one key ingredient that separates for us life from death. As awesome as it is—and as untrustworthy as we are—GOD GAVE EACH OF US THE POWER OF CHOICE.

God gave that power of choice to the Israelites also. Joshua gathered all the tribes to Shechem and relayed the old stories once again so they could recall the great deliverances of God. Even after hearing that God and God alone was the only Deliverer, Israel still had the option to choose or to turn away from the only true God.

> Now therefore fear the Lord, and serve him in sincerity and in truth: and put away the gods which your fathers served on the other side of the flood, and in Egypt; and serve ye the Lord. And if it seem evil unto you to serve the Lord, choose you this day whom ye will serve (Joshua 24:14–15).

"Judy," God said, "this woman who fell had the help given to her that I have given to each of My children. She did not, however, *choose rightly.*"

Choose a Committed Life

Do you know what kept me faithful to Bernie more than any factor? Certainly I would answer first and foremost the fear of the Lord has kept me from sinning. But in his book *The Romance Factor,* Alan Loy McGinnis has summed up my own thoughts:

> The sooner you can make up your mind what you really believe about sexual commitment, the better it will be, because in the long run what you do about having an affair will depend more on your beliefs than on your feelings. The Bible urges fidelity. We are to be true to the mates we have chosen through thick and thin, through periods of sexual excitement and through periods when the excitement is missing.[2]

Now, while you are free from sin's bondage, is the time to formulate your own *Magna Charta* regarding your beliefs on marriage, sexual commitment, and safeguards against sin. It may be a good idea to write down the ideas you have about yourself—your strengths, your weaknesses, and what past experience has taught you. Then, having defined for yourself your own philosophy, fact will take priority over feelings if and when you need to sit down and rethink your stand on lust.

In other words, resolve in your mind as Daniel did *before* a crisis and not *during* a crisis (See Daniel 1:8). Because Daniel resolved previously not to defile himself—but to remain committed regardless of how others behaved—God showed favor to him and helped Daniel stand strong during his time of trial.

A good marriage and remaining committed to your marital partner is no guarantee that you will never "lust after" another, but it is a great defense barrier.

Choose Your First Love

Once you have formed your own Magna Charta about life directions, you need to once again return to your first love—a love for God that is stronger than the love for the sin of the renounced past.

Sometimes when I return home from a full trip of meetings, plane changes, and different time zone schedules, I occasionally fall into what I call a "zombie-period." For the first day or two, I'm too spaced out to do anything but lie on the sofa in my study and hold court for those who need to talk to me. I don't unpack, open mail, or answer phone calls during those few days—I just physically and mentally rest!

Days and days of early rising, late retiring, rushed mealtimes, hours of counseling and sharing, hot lights of TV studios and cold waits at airports absolutely do me in. Because I know the effect this has on me, I evaluate my situation and plan my days accordingly.

In like manner, those who have just returned to God after coming out of sexual bondage are also happy to be "home." Time is needed to re-establish a spiritual rest in your soul.

When I first return home, I'm too beat to even eat. Because of your separation from God, your spiritual appetite for God and His Word may also be diminished.

What I do to renew my physical strength may also be applied to the spiritual life. Come into His presence and sit quietly before Him. Spend as much time in God's presence as you previously had spent on yourself in sin. Rest before Him and allow God to love you.

When I have fully rested and am restored once again, then I can face the normal pressures of my active daily life. My attention span is longer, and I don't growl over little irritations. So, too, will you be able to manage life when you are fully rested in the Lord.

"Thou shalt love the Lord thy God with all thy heart, and with all thy soul, and with all thy mind. . . . And . . . thou shalt love thy neighbor as thyself" (Matthew 22:37,39).

Jesus gave those two commandments in order that they may become our priorities—love God and your neighbor as yourself. The only way they can become priorities is if you return to your first love.

Choose to Believe God

Recently a woman told me she could not break off her relationship with another man because he threatened to tell her husband. I have heard of this threat many times. At first this excuse to stay involved stumped me. What if this other man *would* tell all?

But I believe we can base our decisions on the truth of God's Word.

And we know that all things work together for good to them that love God, to them who are the called according to his purpose. For whom he did foreknow, he also did predestinate to be conformed to the image of his Son, that he might be the firstborn among many brethren (Romans 8:28–29).

My reply to a woman under a threat is this: Do what is right before God. Do not live under the "what ifs." God's will is for you to live in righteousness not unrighteousness. Whatever is around the corner is not worse than what God has promised to those who continue in willful sin.

I have seen God take a threat that became a reality and turn it into a wondrous lesson of His love for His own. God can take what Satan or man meant for evil, and turn it into good. *Threats do not bother God.*

I cannot promise anyone deliverance from the pain of exposure—but God promised deliverance from the pain of separation from Him.

The promise is yours—if you will believe God—and if you will choose rightly.

Standing Tall in the Midst of Trial

A friend recently shared with me a conversation she had with a Christian professor who taught psychology and counseling. They were studying the abnormal choices that people made while under severe stress—withdrawal, depression, alcoholism, bizarre behavior (having an affair), or nervous breakdowns.

This friend went up to her professor after the class and said, "During a five-year span, my father died a horrible death, my mother consoled herself with alcohol, my teenage son took drugs, and my husband had a mid-life crisis. A friend added up my stress points and told me that I topped the chart by 500 points. But I never experienced any of the bizarre behavior that you have mentioned. Continuing to act and think rationally, I took care of each person and still maintained a forty-hour week job myself."

"Why?" he asked.

"Why?" she questioned. "Why? Because no one else would hold down our little fort."

"Wrong," he said. "You had an option to flake out—the same as every other member of your family."

"Well," she said, "maybe it was my faith that kept me going."

"Not entirely," he responded. "Faith is activated by taking a leap from one side of the cliff to another. Your salvation was the fact that you *chose* to be a responsible person—you chose rightly."

He was right. "Faith, if it hath not works, is dead" (James 2:17). Judy's paraphrase: "Faith, without right choices, is also dead."

Maybe some of you reading this book are new in your walk with God. Maybe some of you are not as knowledgeable in the Bible as others are. Maybe some of you are not the prayer warrior God wants you to be. Maybe some of you going through intense trials as my friend was. But all of you can grow in the grace and knowledge of God. And all of you have within you the awesome power of choice!

That power of choice is charged with the same voltage as anyone else's. In this instance, we cannot compare ourselves to any other Christian because we are all equipped the same.

Each of us has the capability to make the correct choice—and experience victory; or we can make the wrong choice—and experience defeat.

Yes, we are complex people living in a complex world. The decisions we make are often complex decisions. Whether you go for counseling or read books on how to stay free from sin, it all boils down to the most simplistic answer God has ever given us:

"Choose ye this day whom ye will serve."

I pray that, having come this far, you will always say no to sin and yes to God, not because you have to, but because *who you really are* wants to.

"The scars of my sin will remain forever. But now they're reminders not only of the mistakes of the past, *but of God's healing and restoration as well.*"
Anonymous (italics added)

Notes

Foreword

1 Hayford, Jack W., Why Sex Sins Are Worse Than Others (Living Way Ministries, Van Nuys, 1989) Used by permission.

2 Stafford, Timothy, Christianity Today (January 10, 1994)

Chapter 1

1 Lewis, C.S., *The Weight of Glory*, (Michigan: Zondervan, 2001)

Chapter 2

1 Lewis, C.S., *Mere Christianity*, (New York: Collier Books, MacMillan Publishing Company, 1960)

2 Meier, Minirth, Wichern. *Introduction to Psychology and Counseling* (Michigan: Baker Book House, 1982), p. 28.

3 Cole, Edwin L. *Maximized Manhood* (Pennsylvania: Whitaker House, 1982), p. 82.

4 McBurney, Louis. "The Avoiding of the Scarlet Letter," *Leadership* (Summer, 1985), p. 44.

5 LaHaye, Tim and Beverly. *The Act of Marriage* (Michigan: Zondervan Publishing House, 1976), p. 46.

6 Cavanaugh, Michael. *God's Call to the Single Adult* (Pennsylvania: Whitaker House, 1986), p. 48.

Chapter 3

1 Stedman, Ray, et al. *Family Life. God's View of Relationships* (Texas: Word, Inc., 1979), p. 187.

Chapter 4

1 Mason, Mike, *The Mystery of Marriage* (Oregon: Multnomah Press, 1985), p. 117.
2 Wright, Norman. *Seasons of a Marriage* (California: Regal Books, 1982), p. 118.
3 Quigley, Pat. "The Unmentionable Temptation," *Virtue* (March April, 1983), p. 42.

Chapter 5

1 Williams, H. Page. *Do Yourself a Favor. Love Your Wife* (New Jersey: Logos International, 1979), p. 15.
2 Hart, Archibald. "Transference: Loosening the Tie That Binds," *Leadership* (Fall, 1982), p. 111.
3 McBurney, Louis. "The Avoiding of the Scarlet Letter," *Leadership* (Summer, 1985), p. 45.
4 White, Mel. *Lust—The Other Side of Love* (New Jersey: Fleming H. Revell Company, 1978), p. 186.

Chapter 6

1 Seamands, David, *Leadership*, (Winter quarter, 1988), p. 23.
2 Osborne, Cecil. *The Art of Understanding Your Mate* (Michigan: Zondervan Publishing House, 1970), p. 223.
3 Hart, Archibald. "Transference: Loosening the Tie That Binds," *Leadership* (Fall, 1982), p. 110.

4 Smith, James. "The Demands, Dilemmas and Dangers of Pastoral Counseling," *Leadership* (Fall, 1980), p. 149.

5 Meier, Paul. "How Self Acceptance Can Help a Marriage," *Christian Life* (May, 1976), p. 22.

Chapter 7

1 Alcorn, Randy, *Leadership*, (Winter quarter, 1988), p. 46.

2 Needham, David. *Birthright* (Oregon: Multnomah Press, 1979), p. 131.

3 McBurney, Louis. "The Avoiding of the Scarlet Letter," *Leadership* (Summer, 1985), p. 49.

4 Dobbins, Richard. "How Far Does Friendship Go?" *Charisma* (May June, 1977), p. 26.

Chapter 8

1 Allender, Dan, *Discipleship Journal*, (August, 1991), p. 28.

2 Harbour, Brian. *Famous Couples of the Bible* (Tennessee: Broadmen Press, 1979), p. 105–106.

3 Clapp, Rodney. "What Hollywood Doesn't Know about Romantic Love," *Christianity Today* (February, 1984), p. 33.

4 Mylander, Charles. *Running the Red Lights* (California: Regal Books, 1986), p. 52.

Chapter 9

1 Santinga, Timothy, *Christian Life*, (May, 1978), p. 19.

2 Meier, Minirith. *Happiness Is a Choice* (Michigan: Baker Book House, 1978), p. 132.

3 Adams, Jay. *Marriage, Divorce, and Remarriage in the Bible* (Michigan: Baker Book House, 1981), p. 53.

Chapter 10

1Lewis, C.S., *The Weight of Glory,* (Zondervan, 2001)

2 Packer, J. I. *Knowing God* (Illinois: InterVarsity Press, 1973), p. 86.

3 Taylor, Howard. *Hudson Taylor's Spiritual Secret* (China Inland Missions, 1935), p. 108.

Chapter 11

1 MacDonald, Gordon. *Rebuilding Your Private World* (Oliver-Nelson Books)

2 McGinnis, Alan L. *The Romance Factor* (California: Harper and Row Publishers, 1982), p. 159–160.

Suggested Reading List

Adams, Jay. *Marriage, Divorce, and Remarriage in the Bible* (Grand Rapids, MI: Baker Book House, 1981).

Chapman, Gary. *Toward a Growing Marriage* (Chicago, IL: Moody Press, 1979).

Daniels, E. J. *I Accuse Kinsey* (Orlando, FL: Christ For The World Publishers, 1954).

Dobson, Dr. James. *What Wives Wish Their Husbands Knew about Women* (Wheaton, IL: Tyndale House Publishers, 1975).

Harbour, Brian L. *Famous Couples of the Bible* (Nashville, TN: Broadman Press, 1979).

LaHaye, Tim and Beverly. *The Act of Marriage* (Grand Rapids, MI: Zondervan Publishing House, 1976).

Lutzer, Erwin W. *Living with Your Passions* (Wheaton, IL: Victor Books, 1983).

Mylander, Charles. *Running the Red Lights* (Ventura, CA: Regal Books, 1986).

Needham, David. *Birthright* (Portland, OR: Multnomah Press, 1979).

Osborne, Cecil. *The Art of Understanding Your Mate* (Grand Rapids, MI: Zondervan Publishing House, 1970).

Packer, J. I. *Knowing God* (Downers Grove, IL: InterVarsity Press, 1973).

Powell, John. *Unconditional Love* (Allen, TX: Argus Communications, 1978).

Schlink, Basilea. *You Will Never Be the Same* (Minneapolis, MN: Bethany Fellowship, Inc., 1972).